CITY TECH

CITY
TECH

20 APPS, IDEAS, AND INNOVATORS
CHANGING THE URBAN LANDSCAPE

ROB WALKER

LINCOLN INSTITUTE
OF LAND POLICY

Cambridge, Massachussetts

Library of Congress Control Number: 2024930849

The columns in this book were originally published in *Land Lines*, the magazine of the Lincoln Institute of Land Policy, between 2015 and 2024.

Designed and composed by Kevin Clarke Design.

Printed and bound by Puritan Press in Hollis, New Hampshire.

♻ Printed on Accent Opaque, an acid-free, FSC-certified, 30 percent post-consumer recycled fiber sheet.

MANUFACTURED IN THE UNITED STATES OF AMERICA

BY KARA SWISHER

Cities have the capability of providing something for everybody,
only because, and only when, they are created by everybody.

—Jane Jacobs, *The Death and Life of Great American Cities*

Let's keep in mind at the start that, even in the midst of the great age of tech, a city is not digital, it is not virtual, it is not made up of bits and bytes, and it is *definitely* not a simulation.

And it will never be thus, no matter how many gadgets we employ or how many doodads we hang off the streetlights or how many cameras or lasers or sensors we embed in it or how fervently we seek to extract data out of the movements of its denizens to render a more efficient world.

That's because a city has been, is, and will always be the sum total of its people, the decidedly human humans in whatever metro region you choose across time and the globe who have built on top of each other over the decades and centuries to create, destroy, and recreate in an endless cycle of innovation.

Speaking of innovation, we are poised for yet another Cambrian explosion when it comes to what cities will morph into. While you might think I am talking about ultra-smart cities or floating sky colonies or even an outpost on Mars that some tech icons like Sergey Brin, Jeff Bezos, and Elon Musk have imagined and pushed forward, what I refer to is much more immediate and realistic. That's important, especially after a pandemic that saw populations fleeing from cities and an acceleration of the trend toward digitally fueled work.

That abrupt shift, of course, has been a shock to municipalities that depend on the tax revenue and, more important, the crowds of workers and residents in downtown areas that keep restaurants and other services humming—and, an added benefit, crime to a minimum. Trying to figure out how to reimagine these lonely urban canyons for new uses is one of the challenges of this time across the world.

Which is why it is so important to think widely about all manner of invention, as Rob Walker adeptly chronicles in this compilation of essays. And there's much more to come: Have you heard of small nuclear devices that will power your house or apartment or workplace? You will. Do you know that advanced AI will be critical in allowing safe and energy-efficient autonomous vehicle fleets to finally work in ways that will fundamentally change how we move around cities? It is close. And those delicious strawberries you just devoured could be coming from an office building near you, with zero dirt involved. It's coming.

Also ripe for change are the kinds of flexible building materials we will employ that are both energy and resource efficient, as well as more affordable and modular ways to build homes, so that nurses and firefighters and teachers can return to live closer to where they work.

And that is only the cities that exist. Right now, in Solano County, California, a group of forward-thinking tech investors are funding and imagining a new city built from scratch. While its secretive purchase of 62,000 acres in the windswept region northeast of overstuffed San Francisco caused some level of controversy in the area, California Forever is aiming to bring more housing to a state, while also trying to avoid the pitfalls of earlier efforts that tried to force create cities where they were not needed or wanted. Whether it succeeds or fails—it is a 20-year bet—will be an interesting experiment to watch. "We're trying to create the walkable, livable cities for everyone since those areas often become too expensive in existing ones," said Jan Sramek to me in a recent interview. "Tech has very little to do with it."

"This City is what it is because our citizens are what they are." It's a recipe for the future that never fails to deliver.

At the same time, data show that two groups, the young and the old, are leading the return to cities after the brief COVID-19 falloff. Both groups are attracted to the many amenities that a city provides, including a more vibrant social scene, better medical care, and cultural opportunities, as well as convenience.

Again, these are human-centered reasons for why cities of the future will thrive. And there is no better example of that than San Francisco, which is starting to see signs of recovery from what many had predicted would be a "doom spiral" of population loss, tax revenue decline, persistent homelessness, and the departure of the tech players who had made it such a digital hub and wealth generator. As it seems to be turning out, in the City by the Bay—which has seen one boom (and bust) after another since its founding—the most recent surge in AI development has sparked another cycle of investment and excitement. That in turn will power what could be a new engine of growth and new ideas on how to work and live, powered by the people and not whatever innovation happens to be waxing or waning.

This is exactly why this book uses the word *innovators* in its title, not *innovations*—and why it tells the stories of the people behind the technologies. It is a sentiment echoed by Plato, who noted about another city in another time long ago: "This City is what it is because our citizens are what they are." It's a recipe for the future that never fails to deliver.

––––––––––––

Kara Swisher is the author of *Burn Book: A Tech Love Story*. She is the host of the podcast *On with Kara Swisher* and was also the cofounder and editor-at-large of *Recode,* host of the *Recode Decode* podcast, and coexecutive producer of the Code conference. Swisher was a former contributing opinion writer for the *New York Times* and host of its *Sway* podcast, and has also worked for the *Wall Street Journal* and the *Washington Post*.

BY ROB WALKER

Cities often seem to evolve gradually, even slowly, a result of how they are planned, used, and replanned. Technology seems to evolve quickly, even restlessly, a result of vision, ambition, and competition.

Both of those characterizations are exaggerated. But they capture the broad-brush tensions—and the opportunities—that have animated the City Tech column since its debut in 2015.

All along, we've looked for examples of experiments, innovators, and projects that balanced the urgency of inventing solutions with the discipline needed to anticipate and accommodate real-world consequences. While the column looked to the possibilities of the future, we strove to ground it in the realities of the present.

For this collection, we selected 20 columns that represent many of the ways emerging technology has shaped cities and urban planning over the past decade, and that introduce you to the people who are devising, embracing, using, studying, and even questioning these new tools and ideas.

Inevitably, not every innovation and experiment documented here achieved its goals; not surprisingly for a sector that prides itself on rapid evolution, promising startups have come and gone, good ideas have been shelved, and new technologies have eclipsed earlier tools. But other projects proved prescient, with many surviving and thriving. And each undertaking documented here sparked progress or inspired fresh insight about possible futures. Looking both back and ahead from the vantage point of the mid-2020s, it's possible to identify some broader, instructive themes in this chronicle of urban technology.

Perhaps the most significant is the importance of collaboration and shared goals that cross traditional lines. Too often, the cities-and-technology narrative in the mainstream press has turned on conflict: the startup "disrupting" not just entrenched business rivals, but also existing policy and planning structures. That does happen, but it's not universal. To the contrary, as described in these pages, companies like Uber and Strava have experimented with municipal partnerships that have the potential to benefit all citizens, not just all customers.

In a similar spirit, a walkability project that started as a guerrilla action morphed into a sanctioned wayfinding pilot in multiple cities, showing how policymakers can embrace activists—and vice versa. Another related, notable trend is the development of tools and services like coUrbanize that aim to revamp and expand citizen participation in that venerable institution, the community planning meeting.

Like many of the stories told here, these examples challenge the stereotype of change-resistant municipal entities. See also the Tennessee utility that led the way in rolling out high-speed internet access to spur broader development in Chattanooga, or the Detroit utility whose embrace of new technology to revamp streetlights became a bright spot in the city's post-bankruptcy history. (In a cautionary reversal of this theme, we also consider how the failure of private and public interests to find a way to align may have doomed an ambitious but flawed smart city proposal in Toronto.)

> We revisited each of the projects, and reconnected with many of the people behind them, to find out what has changed, what challenges remain, and where things are heading next.

Another important theme of the City Tech column has been the steady rise in technology-based efforts to slow both the causes and effects of climate change, the most critical issue facing cities today. Tools like the i-Tree suite developed by the US Forest Service are helping cities quantify the economic benefits of trees—and helping planners and others understand why and where they need to boost the urban canopy. Similarly, precision mapping and data collection tools are guiding infrastructure and land use decisions in the desert West, and new software and apps aimed at architects, landscape architects, and developers are allowing them to better gauge the climate impacts of various design decisions and create more resilient buildings and landscapes. A separate set of tools and projects seeks to wrangle diverse datasets into comprehensible dashboards that local governments can use to understand their emissions and design municipal climate goals.

The related theme of equity has been an important factor in these stories as well. The major investment in electric buses in parts of Latin America, for instance, can have a positive climate impact even as it broadens access to transportation; new initiatives across the United States are promoting e-bikes as a low-carbon transit option while making them more accessible to traditionally underserved communities. Other efforts are encouraging a more sophisticated rethinking of how technology can address and reduce noise pollution—a ubiquitous feature of city life that poses many health risks, especially to those who live near highways, flight paths, and industrial operations—with the same consideration that has been given to making air and water safer.

Finally, City Tech has sought to reveal and explore a newer theme: the ways technology manifests in unexpected contexts. Many people hear the word "technology" and think of datasets and apps and software, but technology isn't just 1s and 0s. Look, for example, to the continued growth of 3D-printed housing, which seemed like a novelty just a few years ago but continues to show surprising momentum and is increasingly being eyed as a solution to the global affordable housing crisis. New approaches to strengthening and deploying the construction material known as mass timber in ambitious building projects reveal how technology can impact something as nondigital as wood. And a growing interest in lowering urban temperatures is sparking innovation in new reflective paints and other "smart surface" materials that can be used on existing roads and rooftops—tools that might not be as glamorous as the latest app or gadget, but that can have immediate and tangible effects.

Throughout the book, these themes overlap, recur, and bump into each other in surprising, and often hopeful, ways.

The book is arranged chronologically, with each column presented as it originally appeared in the Lincoln Institute of Land Policy's _Land Lines_ magazine. Every chapter features additional material, including online resources and newly written updates that bring in the perspectives of today. We revisited each of the projects, and reconnected with many of the people behind them, to find out what has changed, what challenges remain, and where things are heading next.

From the beginning, this column set out to take an expansive view of what city tech, as an idea, could mean. And new answers to that question keep presenting themselves. The story they collectively tell is one that is still very much in progress.

So you can think of this as a book about the intersection of cities and technology, but that familiar metaphor doesn't quite capture the state of things. It feels more like we're approaching a series of busy roundabouts, each with slightly different designs and possibilities. We're on a complicated journey; our decisions can set us off in surprising directions, and opinions may differ on how to navigate the challenges ahead. But based on the examples in this collection, it seems clear that collaboration, creativity, and an openness to new ideas are the keys to getting where we need to go.

These essays originally appeared in *Land Lines*, the magazine of the Lincoln Institute of Land Policy, between 2015 and 2024. Each chapter includes new photos, new resources, and new updates from the people closest to the work.

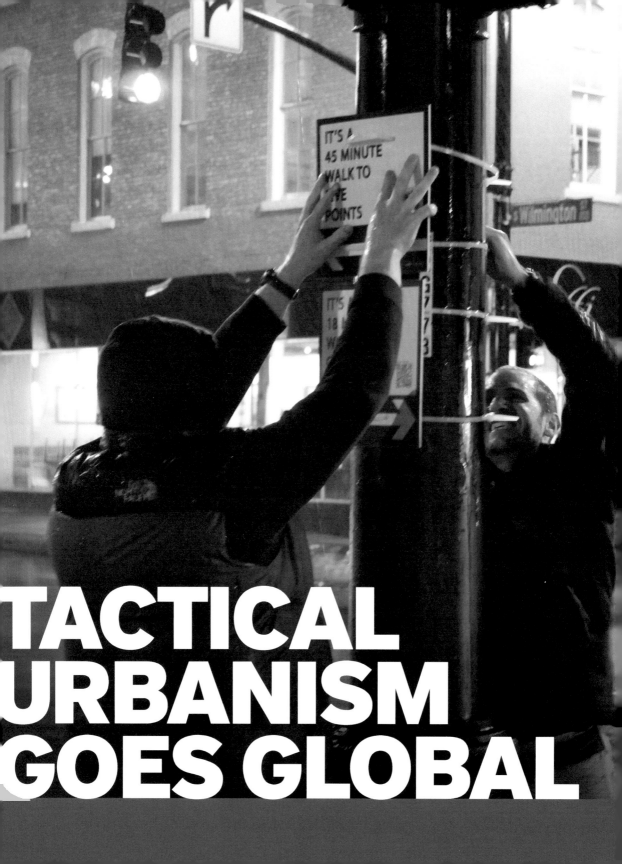

TACTICAL URBANISM GOES GLOBAL

Eager to help more people see how walkable their cities really are, Matt Tomasulo started hanging up signs in the middle of the night.

His grassroots movement became a global platform.

It is a
3 Minute
Walk to
Dinner at San
Pedro Square

Above: Matt Tomasulo, center, started a web-based walkability movement that was embraced by citizens and city officials around the world, including Sal Alvarez (left) and Kim Walesh (right) of the San Jose, California, Office of Economic Development.

Previous: Tomasulo and a friend hang a sign pointing people to Raleigh's Five Points neighborhood. As the Walk [Your City] movement grew, its motto was: "It's not too far."

AS A GRADUATE STUDENT studying urban design and planning, Matt Tomasulo organized a clever wayfinding project to encourage residents of Raleigh, North Carolina, to walk more rather than drive. With a group of confederates, he designed and produced 27 Coroplast signs, each one-foot square, printed with simple messages such as: "It's a 7-Minute Walk to Raleigh City Cemetery," color-coded by destination category, with an arrow pointing the way. The group attached these with zip ties to stoplight poles and the like around three downtown intersections. It took less than 45 minutes to install them all—after dark, because, although the signs looked official, this effort was "unsanctioned," as Tomasulo put it.

As you might expect, the city had the signs taken down. And that could have been the end of it: a provocative gesture and a smart portfolio piece. But in fact, Walk Raleigh underwent an unexpected metamorphosis after it first appeared back in 2012, evolving into Walk [Your City], an ambitious attempt to take the underlying idea nationwide and work with (instead of around) city and planning officials. In 2015, Tomasulo's fledgling organization received a $182,000 grant from the Knight Foundation, sparking a new phase for the project that included a particularly thoughtful series of deployments coordinated with officials in San Jose, California.

This surprising outcome owes much to shrewd uses of technology—and perhaps even more to the input of a handful of planning officials who saw deeper potential in what could have been a fun but ephemeral stunt.

TACTICAL URBANISM GOES GLOBAL

The core of Tomasulo's original insight was to probe and attempt to shift *perceptions* of walking: he'd come upon some interesting research suggesting that people often choose not to walk because a destination simply "feels" farther away than it really is.

Older downtowns such as Raleigh's are often "more walkable than people realize," says Julie Campoli, an urban designer and author of *Made for Walking: Density and Neighborhood Form*, published by the Lincoln Institute of Land Policy. But in many cases, decades of traffic engineering have eroded the sense of walkability in built environments where signage is arranged to be visible to drivers and offers distance information in the car-centric form of miles. For the most part, she says, "the streets are designed for cars."

Tomasulo did his own research in Raleigh, asking neighbors and others if they would, say, walk rather than drive to a certain grocery store if it took 14 minutes. "They'd say, 'Sure, sometimes, at least.' And I'd say: 'Well, it's 12 minutes.' Again and again I had this conversation. People would say, 'I always thought it was too far to walk.'"

This outcome owes much to shrewd uses of technology—and perhaps even more to a handful of planning officials who saw potential in what could have been a fun but ephemeral stunt.

Thus Tomasulo's original signs were oriented to pedestrian eye level, and described distance in terms of minutes to a particular destination of potential interest. Tomasulo documented and promoted the project on Facebook. The enthusiasm there helped attract media attention, culminating in a visit from a BBC video crew.

That's when Tomasulo reached out via Twitter to Mitchell Silver, then Raleigh's planning director and a former president of the American Planning Association. Silver didn't know much about Walk Raleigh, but agreed to talk to the BBC anyway, discussing the desirability of pro-walking efforts and praising this one as a "very cool" example . . . that probably should have gotten a permit first. The clip got even more attention. And when that

Next: The Walk [Your City] project spread to communities of all sizes, including Mount Hope, West Virginia (population 1,100).

Each sign included a QR code for more information about local destinations. QR codes began to be widely used in the United States in the early 2010s; they were invented by a Toyota subsidiary in 1994 to track car parts.

resulted in inquiries about the signs' legality, Silver removed them himself and returned them to Tomasulo.

But Silver also recognized the bigger opportunity. Raleigh's long-term comprehensive plan explicitly called for increasing walkability (and bikeability), an issue that resonated with the fast-growing municipality's notably young population (about 70 percent under age 47 at the time). "It really became a critical thing," he recalls. "Are we going to embrace innovation? Did Walk Raleigh do something wrong or are our codes out of date?" says Silver, who became commissioner of the New York City Department of Parks and Recreation. "Innovation tests regulation. Matt, without realizing it, tested us."

The short-term solution: Tomasulo could donate his signs to the city, which could then reinstall them on an "educational pilot" basis. To help Silver convince the city council, Tomasulo used an online petition to gather 1,255 signatures in three days. The council unanimously approved the return of Walk Raleigh.

Tomasulo pushed a little further. Raising $11,364 on Kickstarter, he and partners built WalkYourCity.org, which offers customizable signage templates to anyone, anywhere. This has led to more than 100 communities creating citizen-led projects in large and small municipalities across the United States and beyond.

That shouldn't be a surprise, given what Campoli describes as a growing interest in walkability among citizens and planners alike. The smart growth movement has revived interest in compact city forms, she says, "and in the last 10 years, that has converged in this idea of walkability." Key demographic groups—millennials and empty nesters, particularly—have recognized that car culture is "not as wonderful as it was made out to be," she observes.

And there's an economic dimension for cities, she adds. One way to gauge that is through growing real-estate values associated with more compact, walkable forms.

The economic impact factor inspired a collaboration with officials in San Jose, which stands out as an example of how tactical urbanism can influence real-world planning. Sal Alvarez, of the city's Office of Economic Development, was a fan of WalkYourCity. org as an open online platform—but pointed out that "the city will probably come take the signs down," he says. "You need a champion on the inside, really." He and Jessica Zenk of the city's Department of Transportation served that role in San Jose, quickly launching three pilot programs.

Each was concentrated and strategic. The first leveraged the popularity of the San Pedro Square Market, a concentration of restaurants and businesses in the city's two-square-mile downtown. It's a favored local destination, but the sort that people often drive to and from without exploring. So a set of 47 signs pointed to nearby attractions like the adjacent Little Italy district, a park with extensive walking trails, the arena where the city's National Hockey League team plays, and a second park that has been the focus of ongoing revitalization efforts. A second downtown project involved recruiting a dozen volunteers to help put up 74 signs meant to draw links between the city's SoFa arts district and landmarks within walking distance, like the convention center.

Participants in a Walk [Your City] campaign organized by Creative Santa Fe, a nonprofit in New Mexico that drives positive change through community events and collaborations.

Tomasulo documented and promoted the project on Facebook. The enthusiasm there helped attract media attention, culminating in a visit from a BBC video crew.

The popularity of these two experiments inspired a city council member to propose the third, set in a neighborhood outside the downtown core. This centered on a road being converted from four lanes to two, with a middle turn lane and bike lane to enable a shift away from vehicle travel.

Tomasulo—now armed with a master's in city and regional planning from the University of North Carolina at Chapel Hill and another in landscape

BUILD A SIGN

1 2 3 4 5 **6** 7

Shops / Restaurants / Neighborhood Centers

...is this?

Commercial | Public Space

Civic / Institutional | Amusement

Transit | Custom

Continue

IT IS AN 11 MINUTE WALK TO A NEIGHBORHOOD GROCERY

Right: Sign-building instructions on the Walk [Your City] website.

Opposite: A member of the Charleston, South Carolina, sign-hanging crew.

architecture from North Carolina State University—has added a new batch of color-coded sign designs that point specifically to other car-alternative infrastructure, including bike-share locations and Caltrain stops. The city has been gathering traffic data for this project that may help measure the impact of these 50 or so signs at 12 intersections. To Alvarez, the signs are useful in pushing the cultural changes that help infrastructure shifts take hold.

More broadly, San Jose officials worked with Tomasulo to "put some tools in the toolbox" of Walk [Your City] to encourage and help enthusiasts to find their own champions within local municipalities, so these projects can contribute to the planning process. "If you don't get the city to buy in at some point," Campoli says, "you're not going to get that permanent change that a short-term event is intended to lead to."

Back in Raleigh, the original project is evolving into a permanent feature of the landscape, with fully vetted and planned campaigns in four neighborhoods, and a partnership with Blue Cross/Blue Shield. That's a solid example of what Silver advocated: a city embracing a grassroots urbanism project instead of just regulating.

But the San Jose example is showing how much the reverse proposition matters, too: tactical urbanism can benefit from embracing official planning structures. Tomasulo certainly sounds pleased with his project's transition from "unsanctioned" experiment to active partnerships with insiders in San Jose and elsewhere. He uses a term he picked up for officials whose enthusiasm, creativity, and practical how-to-get-it-done wisdom cuts against an all-too-common stereotype. "They're not bureaucrats," he says. "They're herocrats." ❯

THE LATEST

Walk [Your City] grew from a grassroots effort to encourage people to walk more in Raleigh, North Carolina, into a global phenomenon that inspired more than 700 campaigns to encourage walkability in 50-plus countries. A month after this column was published, WalkYourCity.org founder and self-described "civic instigator" Matt Tomasulo was appointed to the Raleigh Planning Commission; he served for six years, including a stint as chair. After undertaking a preservation project converting a historic Raleigh home into a boutique inn, he and his wife have focused on other hospitality projects in walkable areas and on "missing middle" housing opportunities, building on his planning commission experience encouraging walkability. WalkYourCity.org ended operations in 2016, but thanks to a Knight Foundation grant, Tomasulo developed a toolkit that helped spark awareness of opportunities for walkability around the world. "Walkability is a part of the conversation now, in a way that it was not" a decade ago, Tomasulo says. "Connectivity for nonmotorized travel seems to finally have a permanent seat at the table."

LEARN MORE

Made for Walking: Density and Neighborhood Form (Lincoln Institute of Land Policy)
https://www.lincolninst.edu/publications/books/made-walking

Walk Score
https://www.walkscore.com

The 20-Minute Suburb (Skidmore, Owings & Merrill)
https://www.som.com/research/the-20-minute-suburb

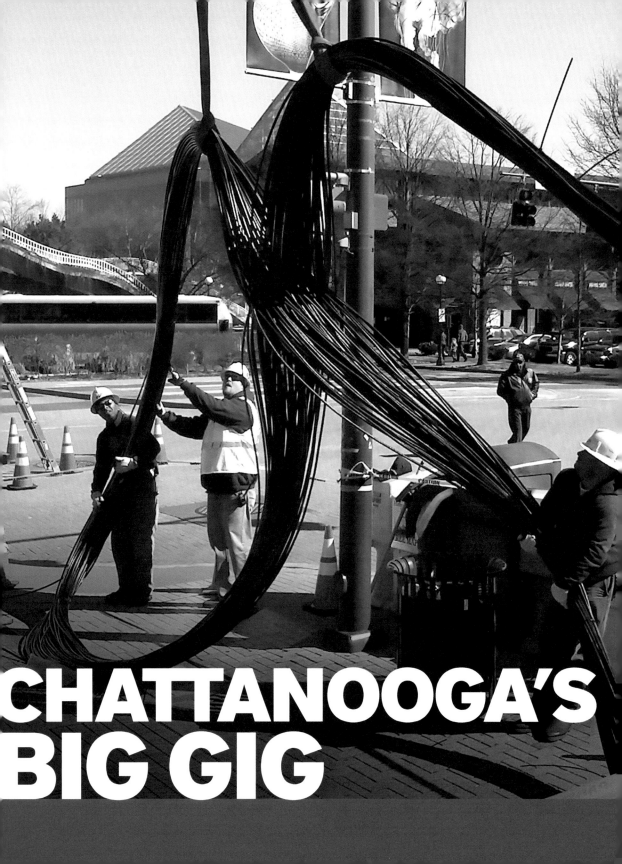

CHATTANOOGA'S BIG GIG

Can access to high-speed internet help revitalize a downtown?

Leaders in Chattanooga bet yes—years before the pandemic caused many other cities to scramble to attract tech-savvy remote workers.

Above: A meeting of Tech Goes Home Chattanooga, which provides computers, internet access, and skills training to help bridge the digital divide. The launch of the initiative was inspired by the city's investments in high-speed internet.

Previous: Workers install fiber-optic cable in Chattanooga as part of an effort by the local utility, EPB, to upgrade internet access citywide.

UNIVERSAL HIGH-SPEED INTERNET ACCESS is a popular dream these days—everyone from the president to Google has embraced it. And the tech press is full of testy critiques wondering why typical broadband speeds in the United States lag so far behind those in, say, South Korea.

Just five years ago, this wasn't such a hot topic. Back then, the discussion—and action—wasn't led by the federal government or the private sector. The first movers were diverse but forward-thinking municipalities: cities and towns like Chattanooga, Tennessee; Lafayette, Louisiana; Sandy, Oregon; and Opelika, Alabama.

Motives and solutions varied, of course. But as high-speed connectivity is becoming recognized as crucial civic infrastructure, Chattanooga provides a useful case study. Its journey to self-proclaimed "Gig City" status—referring to the availability of internet connections with 1 gigabit-per-second data transfer speeds, up to 200 times faster than the typical broadband speed for many Americans—started with a visionary municipal initiative, built upon via thoughtful private and public coordination. Most recently, this effort has even begun to tangibly affect city planning and development, particularly in the form of an in-progress reimagining of a long-sleepy downtown core. In short, Chattanooga is starting to answer a vital question: once a city has world-class internet access, what do you actually *do* with it?

The journey to "Gig City" status started with a visionary municipal initiative. This effort even began to tangibly affect city planning and development.

The story began more than a decade ago, when Chattanooga's city-owned electric utility, EPB, was planning a major upgrade to its power grid. Its CEO, Harold Depriest, argued for a plan that involved deploying fiber-optic cable that could also be used for internet access. After clearing local regulatory hurdles, the new system was built out by 2010, and every EPB power customer in the Chattanooga area—meaning pretty much every home or business—had gigabit access. But you had to pay for it, just like electricity. And the early pricing for the fastest access was about $350 a month.

"They had very, very few takers," recalls Ken Hays, president of the Enterprise Center, a nonprofit that since 2014 has focused, at the behest of local elected officials, on strategizing around what Chattanoogans call "the gig." The head of Lamp Post Group, a successful local tech-focused venture firm, made a point of signing up immediately, Hays continues. But on a citywide level, "we didn't have the excitement" that gig-level access generates today. And in 2010, he adds, "there weren't many good case studies out there."

But broader change was afoot. The announcement of Google Fiber—the internet search giant's foray into building out high-speed online infrastructure—sparked new interest. And in 2013, Jenny Toomey, a Ford Foundation director focused on internet rights, helped organize a summit of sorts where officials from municipalities like Chattanooga, Lafayette, and elsewhere could meet and compare notes.

"It was still pretty nascent at the time," recalls Lincoln Institute President and CEO George W. McCarthy, an economist who was then director of metropolitan opportunity at the Ford Foundation.

A technician at EPB, which has remained on the tech cutting edge, unveiling the country's first 10-gigabit broadband service in 2015, the first communitywide 25-gigabit service in 2022, and the first commercially available quantum network in 2022.

But that summit, he continues, helped spark new conversations about how such initiatives can make cities more competitive and more equitable, and less reliant on the purely private-sector solutions we often assume are more efficient than government ones. "And over the course of two years since, this issue has just exploded," he says.

In fact, that summit turned out to be the rare event that actually spawned a new organization: Next Century Cities, founded in 2014, quickly attracted more than 100 member municipalities. They share best practices around an agenda that treats high-speed internet access as a fundamental, nonpartisan infrastructure issue that communities can and should control and shape.

Chattanooga's embrace of its "Gig City" identity spurred significant investments in its downtown, including the $9.5 million conversion of a partially abandoned 19th century hotel (top) into the Tomorrow Building (bottom), a mixed-use co-living space developed for remote workers.

Against this backdrop, Chattanooga was taking steps to demonstrate how "the gig" could be leveraged. The Lamp Post Group had moved into downtown space, and superlative internet access was just a starting point for the young, tech-savvy workers and entrepreneurs it wanted to attract. "If we don't have housing, if we don't have open space, if we don't have cool coffee shops—they're going to go to cities that have all that," says Kim White, president and CEO of nonprofit development organization River City Company.

Starting in 2013, a city-center plan and market study conducted by River City proposed strategies to enhance walkability, bikeability, green space, and—especially—housing options. More than 600 people participated in the subsequent planning process, which ultimately targeted 22 buildings for revitalization or demolition. Today, half of those are being redeveloped, says White, and more than $400 million has been invested downtown; in the next year and a half, 1,500 apartments will be added to the downtown market, plus new student housing and hotel beds.

The city has provided tax incentives, some of which are designed to keep a certain percentage

of the new housing stock affordable. Leaders have also invested $2.8 million in a downtown park that's a "key" part of the plan, White continues, to "have areas where people can come together and enjoy public space." One of the apartment projects, the Tomorrow Building, will offer "micro-units" and a street-level restaurant. "I don't think we would have attracted these kinds of businesses and younger people coming to look," without the gig/tech spark, White concludes. "It put us on the map."

The gig was also the inspiration for a city-backed initiative identifying core development strategies that led to the Enterprise Center pushing a downtown "innovation district," says Hays. Its centerpiece involves making over a 10-story office building into the Edney Innovation Center, featuring coworking spaces as well as the headquarters of local business incubator CO.LAB. The University of Tennessee at Chattanooga has a project involving a 3D printer lab in the Innovation District, and even the downtown branch of the Chattanooga Public Library has been made over to include a tech-centric education space.

EPB, whose original fiber-optic vision set the Gig City idea in motion, has long since figured out more workable pricing schemes—gig access now starts at about $70 a month—and drawn more than 70,000 customers. It has also offered qualified low-income residents 300-megabit access,

Above: Two-acre Miller Park is at the center of a downtown innovation district established in 2014, part of the city's efforts to foster a culture of entrepreneurship and experimentation.

Next: Illustrating the ripple effect of the city's investments in technology, a professor from Southern Adventist University demonstrates a fundamental principle of quantum physics for middle-school students in the Chattanooga suburb of Collegedale. The event took place during World Quantum Day in 2023.

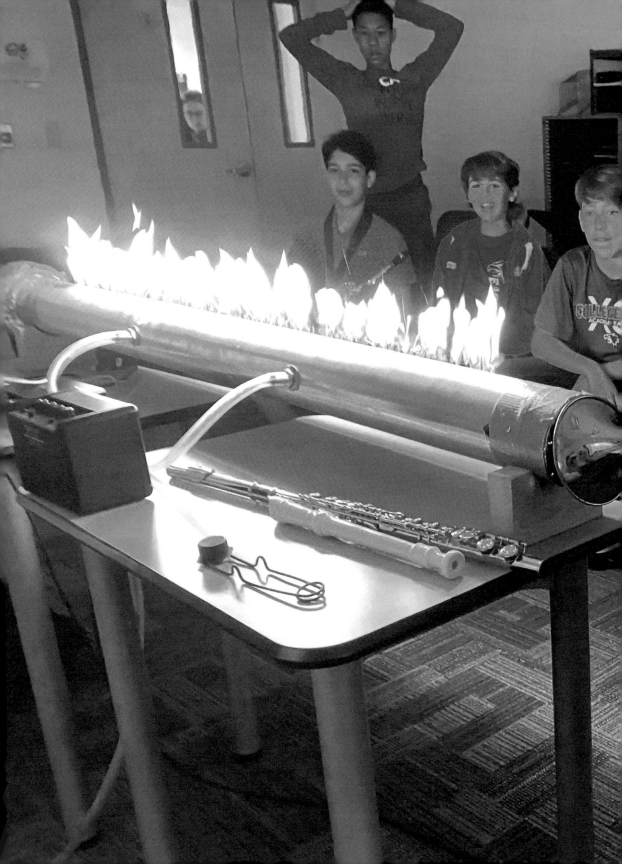

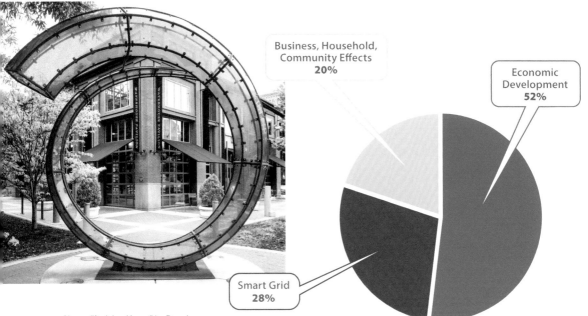

Business, Household, Community Effects **20%**

Economic Development **52%**

Smart Grid **28%**

Above: "Arriving Home," by Dennis Oppenheim, graces Miller Plaza in Chattanooga's innovation district (left); a 2020 study estimated the total economic impact of the city's internet investments at $2.7 billion, or $646 per resident, across several key categories (right).

Opposite: Quantum network servers, managed in a partnership between EPB and Qubitekk.

which is still much faster than most broadband in the United States, for reduced rates. And its efforts to expand into underserved areas adjacent to Chattanooga have become an important component of broader efforts to challenge regulations in many states, from Texas to Minnesota to Washington, that effectively restrict municipalities from building their own high-speed access solutions.

In short, a lot has changed—in Chattanooga and in other cities and towns that have pushed for internet infrastructure that the private sector wasn't providing. "Most of this work right now is happening at the local level," says Debra Socia, who heads Next Century Cities. "It's mayors and city managers and CIOs taking the steps to figure out what their city needs." The implications for crucial civic issues from education to health care to security are still playing out. And precisely because the thinking and planning is happening on a municipal level, it won't be driven solely by market considerations that favor what's profitable instead of what's possible. "It's a both/and argument," McCarthy says. "That's the beauty of it." ❯

Because the thinking and planning is happening on a municipal level, it won't be driven solely by market considerations that favor what's profitable instead of what's possible.

THE LATEST

In its first decade of operation, Chattanooga's fiber-optic network generated $2.7 billion in economic benefits, according to EPB. Early in the pandemic, a partnership including EPB, area governments and schools, and the nonprofit Enterprise Center collaborated to provide schoolchildren from low-income households with high-speed home access at no cost to the family, says Debra Socia, who became president of the Enterprise Center in 2019 and announced her retirement in 2024. Today, the program provides home access with upload and download speeds of at least 300 megabits per second to an estimated 30,000 people. As the nation continues to invest in expanding high-speed broadband–the 2021 infrastructure bill included $42 billion to make access universal across the United States by 2030—EPB is busy betting on the next big thing: the utility launched the country's first commercially available quantum computing network in 2022 and announced the Collaborative for Energy Resilience and Quantum Science with Oak Ridge National Laboratory in 2024.

LEARN MORE

Gig City (City of Chattanooga)
https://chattanoogacalling.com/work/gig

Broadband Commission for Sustainable Development
https://www.broadbandcommission.org/universal-connectivity

Quantum Computing (CalTech)
https://scienceexchange.caltech.edu/topics/quantum-science-explained/
quantum-computing-computers

GET ENGAGED: PLANNING MOVES ONLINE

Long before the pandemic made virtual meetings a necessity, planner Karin Brandt and data scientist David Quinn imagined a world where

people could participate in community planning processes from the comfort of their own homes.

Above: A coUrbanize sign invites public engagement during a redevelopment process in Cambridge, Massachusetts.

Previous: The developers of Innovation QNS—a five-block revitalization project in Astoria, Queens—partnered with coUrbanize to reach more than 31,000 neighborhood residents online, gathering hundreds of comments to present to the New York City Council.

AFTER KARIN BRANDT FINISHED HER MASTER'S DEGREE at the Massachusetts Institute of Technology, she noticed some frustration among her former classmates in planning. "The idea of creating change that we talked about in grad school wasn't being realized," she recalls. One of the reasons was that the process of engaging with the broader public often proved to be a challenge.

Meanwhile, she continues, friends from other MIT departments were "starting companies, solving problems, doing really interesting things" with technology. Perhaps, she concluded, there was a useful overlap in these two divergent trends. Maybe innovative technology could be used to improve some public-facing elements of the planning process. So in 2013, after leaving a position as a research analyst at the Lincoln Institute of Land Policy, Brandt founded coUrbanize with data scientist and fellow MIT grad David Quinn. The venture-backed startup offers a planning-centric communications platform, designed to ease and enhance the way planners, developers, and the public engage with specific projects.

The underlying challenge here was, of course, familiar to anyone involved in the profession. "The traditional planning meeting, with the microphone, and the sign-up list, and three minutes per speaker, is important," says

Only some members of a community have the time or inclination to participate in traditional planning meetings—resulting in a limited perspective on what a community really thinks about a development or planning initiative, leaving potentially useful feedback and input unexpressed.

Amy Cotter, a veteran of Boston's Metropolitan Area Planning Council who is now manager of urban sustainability at the Lincoln Institute. "But it's of limited value." In short, only some members of a community have the time or inclination to participate in such forums—resulting in a limited perspective on what a community really thinks about a development or planning initiative, leaving potentially useful feedback and input unexpressed.

In the past, some treated this step of the planning process as "a more technical exercise" that privileged expert data over community input, Cotter continues. "But the planning field has been undergoing a transition. At this point, most planners feel their plans are richer and better if people are engaged." But securing that engagement is easier said than done.

Ken Snyder, founder and CEO of the Denver-based nonprofit PlaceMatters, observes that, over the past five or 10 years, there has been a growing movement around innovation that increases community engagement, and it very much includes new technologies. Urban Interactive Studio's EngagingPlans platform is one example. Another is CrowdGauge.org—developed by Sasaki Associates and PlaceMatters. The latter is an "open-source, web-based tool for creating educational online games" that can help "summarize, communicate, and rank ideas that emerge from visioning processes and incorporate them into decision-making."

Brandt says her own research led her to conclude that the three major actors in most projects—planners, developers, and the community at large—really all sought the same thing: more transparency from the other two parties. In other words, as much as planners wanted more public input, citizens often felt they weren't getting enough information in a truly accessible form.

Next: Public input on the coUrbanize platform helped JBG SMITH shape elements of National Landing, a 150-acre neighborhood redevelopment project in Arlington and Alexandria, Virginia, that is home to Amazon HQ2.

Below: Karin Brandt and David Quinn founded coUrbanize in 2013. Brandt is now the company's CEO; Quinn is at Google Maps.

CoUrbanize helped publicize and gather feedback on early plans for Karam Senior Living, a project that combines a branch of the Cleveland Public Library with 51 affordable residential units.

CoUrbanize was developed with direct input from planners and developers, and the platform provides a central online home for public information on any given project. That means it serves as both a forum for community feedback and as a spot where plans and proposals are made widely accessible. And the tool aims to be a flexible touchpoint that supplements, but does not replace, real-world feedback mechanisms, both traditional and otherwise.

One of the most interesting examples so far has involved the Kendall Square Urban Renewal Plan in Cambridge, Massachusetts. The Cambridge Redevelopment Authority and developer Boston Properties collaborated on a public-private effort that entailed a million square feet of new commercial and residential development. Working with coUrbanize, the developer distributed poster-style signage asking real-world users of the space for thoughts on its potential uses. This meant anyone could text in their answers, which were collected in an online coUrbanize community forum.

"People have much more interesting ideas when they're in a physical space," Brandt says. "And most people don't know what they can say. So prompting them with specific questions really helps." The exercise drew more than 200 comments, plus additional data from forum users supporting or disagreeing with those comments. The planning and development team "made changes to their plan, based on feedback," Brandt says—including the addition of more substantial affordable housing, and the inclusion of "innovation space" that offered below-market rates to qualified

Developed with direct input from planners and developers . . .
it serves as both a forum for community feedback, and as a
spot where plans and proposals are made widely accessible.

startups. Work on some of the ideas for open space that evolved on the
platform will be underway soon, she adds.

The key here from a planning perspective is to broaden the range of input.
Maybe that means hearing an idea that would never have surfaced in a traditional community meeting. But more important, arguably, is a clearer sense
of what "the community" around a particular project—not just the people
who turn up at a public meeting—really wants, supports, or objects to.

Cotter points out—and Brandt emphatically agrees—that those in-person
hearings still matter. But a platform like coUrbanize provides a forum for
people who can't (or just don't want to) show up for such gatherings: a
worker with a night shift, parents who need to be home during a scheduled
meeting, or millennials who just find the online context easier and more
convenient. "One of our clients calls us a 24-hour community meeting,"
Brandt says. Notably, coUrbanize includes community guidelines that
require citizen-users to register with their real names, which has minimized
the planning-feedback equivalent of spam. "We hear from our municipal
partners that the feedback they get on coUrbanize is often a lot more on
point," Brandt says.

To make the most of this accessibility,
cities or developers using coUrbanize
or any such platform must give fresh
thought to how they present their ideas.
As Cotter notes, even basic terms like
"setback" or "density" may mean little to
a layperson. (As a prompt for community
feedback, PlaceMatters has used such
creative means as a "pop-up" installation to demonstrate the benefits of a
protected bike lane in Portland, Oregon,
in real, physical space.) CoUrbanize offers
planners and developers an intuitive tem-
plate for presenting ideas in both images
and words—almost like a Kickstarter
campaign's home page.

The pandemic made virtual meetings
a necessity, creating new avenues for
public participation.

"A lot more people are online than those who are available at seven o'clock on a Tuesday night."

Of course, it's really up to users to make the most of the platform. And because the coUrbanize business model depends in part on developers signing on, Brandt emphasizes that this sort of platform can more quickly and efficiently reveal problems that under normal circumstances could have led to costly project delays. Most of the firm's early clients and projects are concentrated in Massachusetts, but it has also worked with others in Atlanta and elsewhere who have sought out coUrbanize, and the firm has expanded its focus to cities including New York and San Francisco.

Opposite: The Washington, DC, Office of Planning sets up shop at a street festival in 2022, part of an effort to prioritize equity and increase engagement.

Below: Exploring plans for coastal resilience at a public planning meeting in Chesapeake, Virginia.

The ideal is a "win win win," as Brandt puts it—benefiting all players. Certainly, the potential payoff for actual community members—not only users of coUrbanize, but also people involved in other efforts to broaden the planning process with technological tools—is particularly intriguing. And, as Cotter says, that is something planners have sought for years, and it's becoming more plausible as technologies improve.

The key, she says, is to "give people the confidence that they've been heard, and that their input will be considered." Even if that input isn't followed, it should be made clear what tradeoffs were involved and why.

"So many people don't know that they can shape their neighborhoods," Brandt says. "They don't know what planning is, and they've never been to a meeting." Maybe the current wave of tech-driven platforms can help change that. After all, Brandt argues, "A lot more people are online than those who are available at seven o'clock on a Tuesday night." ❯

THE LATEST

The software-and-strategy organization Karin Brandt and David Quinn created, coUrbanize, has now worked on more than 550 development and planning initiatives in 31 US states and Canada, expanding beyond real estate and planning projects to everything from public art plans to nuclear reactors. And while the pandemic made virtual planning processes more commonplace, Brandt notes that increasing public engagement involves a lot more than setting up a Zoom link. "Since the pandemic," she says, "project teams have found that virtual community meetings are not the 'silver bullet' that many expected for expanding engagement." While virtual meetings opened up new conversations about community accessibility, they only hinted at the potential for technology to enable wider engagement, Brandt says: "The opportunity for project leaders to earn broad support is in finding and activating people who don't know about their project, but would support it, outside of public meetings."

LEARN MORE

coUrbanize
https://www.courbanize.com

CrowdGauge
http://crowdgauge.org

Virtual Engagement Resources for Municipal Staff (Metropolitan Area Planning Council)
https://www.mapc.org/wp-content/uploads/2022/01/Virtual-Engagement-Toolbox_Final.pdf

IN CASE OF EMERGENCY
↓ PULL DOWN ↓

IN CASE OF EMERG
↓ PULL DOWN ↓

EMERGENCY EXIT

PRIORITY
SEATING

EMERGENCY EXIT

RIDE-SHARING AND PUBLIC TRANSIT MEET

The sudden and disruptive rise of ride-sharing created an uneasy relationship with many cities and policymakers.

So it was notable when officials in Altamonte Springs, Florida, launched the nation's first public-private partnership with Uber, integrating the service into the region's public transportation options.

FOR YEARS, it looked like the next big thing in public transportation for the suburban city of Altamonte Springs, Florida, would be an innovative program called FlexBus. Instead of running on fixed routes, buses would respond to demand from kiosks located at specific activity centers. It was, city manager Frank Martz says, "the first demand-response transportation project ever developed in the United States." Some even referred to it as an "Uber for transit."

Unfortunately, it didn't work out. The regional bus operator administering the plan lost key federal funding, and Altamonte Springs had to look for a new solution. "Rather than be mad," Martz continues, "we decided to solve the problem. We still needed to serve our residents."

Most of what we hear about the relationship between municipalities and ride-sharing startups involves contention. But Altamonte Springs is an example of how some cities, planners, and scholars are trying to find opportunities.

This time, officials went with Uber itself. In March 2016, the Orlando suburb announced a straightforward partnership with the ride-sharing firm, subsidizing citizens who opted to use that service instead of their own cars—particularly for trips to regional rail stations that connect population centers around Seminole County. The pilot proved popular enough that several municipalities in the area launched similar programs.

Most of what we hear about the relationship between municipalities and ride-sharing startups involves contention. Right around the time Altamonte Springs started this pilot program, a standoff over regulatory details in Austin, Texas, led both Uber and its chief rival Lyft to stop doing business in the city.

Previous: View from a SunRail car departing Altamonte Springs for Orlando. Several cities along the 49-mile route agreed to help residents pay for Uber rides to and from SunRail stations.

But Altamonte Springs is an example of how some cities, planners, and scholars are trying to find opportunities within the rise of ride-sharing's prominence and popularity. MIT's Senseable City Lab has worked with Uber; UC Berkeley's Transportation Sustainability Research Center and others have been diving into ride-sharing data with an eye toward public transportation impacts. And the American Public Transportation

Valley Regional Transit, the public transit agency in Boise, Idaho, has made low-cost Lyft rides available to residents since 2019. The program recently expanded from 15 eligible bus stops to 70. Cities across the United States have partnered with ride-sharing companies to offer reduced costs for residents connecting to public transit.

"The focus could not and should not be on infrastructure. It needed to be on human behavior."

Association released a study assessing how new services can complement more familiar forms of "shared mobility," and suggested ways that agencies can "promote useful cooperation between public and private mobility providers."

"What it's going to boil down to is how this new system interacts with the existing, traditional system," says Daniel Rodriguez, a Lincoln Institute fellow who teaches planning at the University of North Carolina and has studied transportation innovation in Latin America and the United States. He expects more experiments as cities work to figure out how "to get Uber users to complement the existing infrastructure."

That almost exactly describes one of the prime motivations for the Uber pilot in Altamonte Springs: the service was, Martz points out, an existing option that required none of the time-and-money commitments associated with a typical transportation initiative. "The focus could not and should not be on infrastructure," he said. "It needed to be on human behavior." In other words, ride-sharing services already respond to demand that has been demonstrated by the market, so how could the city hitch a ride on that trend?

Uber began incorporating public transit options into its app in 2019.

The answer was to offer local users a subsidy: the city would pay 20 percent of the cost of any local ride, and 25 percent for rides to or from

   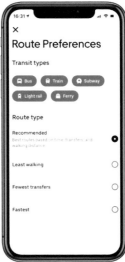

SunRail stations, the region's commuter-rail system. Riders simply entered a code that worked in concert with Uber's "geofencing" technology to confirm location eligibility; their fee was lowered accordingly, and the city seamlessly made up the difference. "It's all about user convenience," Martz says. But he's getting at a bigger point than ease of payment. Instead of building systems that citizens respond to, maybe it's worth trying a system that responds to where citizens actually are—and adjusts in real time as that changes.

Whether this works out in the long run remains to be seen, but as an experiment the risks are pretty low. Martz has estimated the annual cost to the city at about $100,000—compared to $1.5 million for the earlier FlexBus plan. While the pilot is just a few months old, he says local Uber use has risen tenfold—which is why neighboring municipalities Longwood, Lake Mary, Sanford, and Maitland have all joined in or announced plans to do so. ("We're creating a working group among our cities," Martz adds, with a focus on managing traffic congestion and "how to connect our cities.")

As Rodriguez points out, the land use implications alone, both short- and long-term, are compelling. On the day-to-day level, affordable ride-sharing as an option for, say, doctor visits or school appointments or similar

Above: Passengers at the SunRail station in Longwood, one of the communities that participated in the ride-sharing pilot.

Next: A SunRail train travels through nearby Winter Park.

errands lowers demand for parking spaces. On a higher level, it leverages options that already exist instead of devising more land-intensive projects that can take years to plan and complete.

In a sense, the experiment fits into a broader trend of seeking ad hoc transportation innovations. Rodriguez has studied experiments from home-grown bus systems to aerial trams in Latin America that supplemented existing systems rather than building new ones. And while at first blush the concept of partnering with a ride-sharing service sounds like something that would work only in a smaller municipality that lacks a realistic mass transit option, he points out that it could actually play a role in bigger cities. One example: São Paulo, Brazil, which offers what CityLab has called "the best plan yet for dealing with Uber"—essentially auctioning off credits, available to both existing taxi services and ride-sharing upstarts, to drive a certain number of miles in a set time period. The regulatory details (devised in part by former Lincoln Institute fellow Ciro Biderman) aim to give the city options, while capturing and exploiting market demand rather than trying to shape it.

That captures Martz's broader attitude. "Why," he asks, "should the public sector focus on infrastructure embraced by people who used it 40 years ago?" While he readily notes that this line of policy thinking is very much in step with the county's pro-free-enterprise attitudes, he also notes that local political support for the plan crossed party lines. And more significantly, he stresses that this solution leaves the city much more easily positioned to adjust as technology changes. Carpooling scenarios seem like one logical possibility. And Uber and other technology companies are known to be working on driverless-car scenarios that could prove even more efficient. Martz doesn't quite come out and say this, but if Uber gets "disrupted" by some more efficient solution, striking up a new partnership would be a lot easier than a do-over on a multiyear region-wide project. "Let market forces carry the day," Martz says.

Opposite: The city of São Paulo, Brazil, has pioneered regulatory approaches to ride-sharing.

Below: During the second year of the Florida pilot, the five participating cities subsidized more than 185,000 Uber rides, covering 25 percent of the cost of rides to and from SunRail stations.

The combination of uncertainty and potential is exactly why it's worth attending to efforts that embrace ride-sharing upstarts instead of fighting them.

Of course, as Rodriguez notes, all of this remains very experimental at this stage—and a full-on embrace of ride-sharing carries potential downsides. It obviously remains car-centric and not necessarily affordable to broad swaths of many city populations, even with the 20 percent discount. The ability to travel longer distances for lower costs has been a major factor in city sprawl. "This could be another step in that direction," he observes.

But the combination of uncertainty and potential is exactly why it's worth attending to efforts that embrace ride-sharing upstarts instead of fighting them. "There's no correct answer right now; it's still an exploration," Rodriguez cautions. But the likes of Uber do offer one attribute that's hard to deny for those willing to experiment, he adds: "It's tangible, and you know it works." ❯

Opposite: In 2023, the city of Altamonte Springs began testing an autonomous shuttle to provide a new first- and last-mile transportation option.

Below: By 2018, partnerships between public transit agencies and ride-sharing companies had spread across the country.

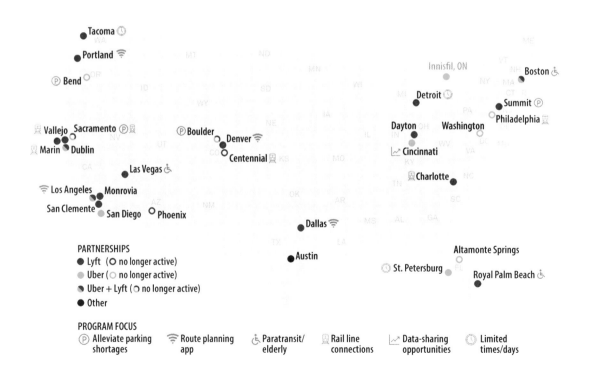

THE LATEST

The Altamonte Springs experiment ended as planned in 2018, but Uber has expanded its partnerships with various public transit agencies, boasting an estimated 30 or more by 2022. Though none has broken through as a replicable success, opportunity remains—particularly given the challenges to transit systems brought on by the pandemic. "Although public-private transit experiments peaked a couple of years ago, their lessons and usefulness are probably most relevant today," says Daniel Rodriguez, director of the Institute of Transportation Studies and professor at the University of California, Berkeley. "With many transit agencies in the US and elsewhere facing a significant fiscal cliff, a dramatic reorientation of transit service is in order." Transit apps can play a role in both low- and high-density environments, Rodriguez notes: "In some cities in low- and middle-income countries, we are seeing the emergence of new apps developed by and for informal and semi-formal transportation services such as tuk-tuks, three-wheelers, and motorcycle taxis. These are exciting developments because they are democratizing the benefits of these apps, while allowing for the delivery of very targeted subsidies—in Bangalore, for example, women are riding for free." Meanwhile, Uber has incorporated public transit information into its own app, and Altamonte Springs continues to embrace innovative mobility plans: the city built a "multimodal flex path" in 2023 and introduced an autonomous shuttle route for first-mile and last-mile trips.

LEARN MORE **Transportation Sustainability Research Center** (UC Berkeley)
https://tsrc.berkeley.edu

Can Uber-Like Public Transit Replace Old-Fashioned Buses? (*Stateline*)
https://stateline.org/2022/08/17/can-uber-like-public-transit-replace-old-fashioned-buses

American Public Transportation Association
https://www.apta.com

DOCKLESS BIKE-SHARING GAINS SPEED

Bike-share systems were already on the rise in the mid 2010s, when Chinese enterprises including Mobike and ofo rolled out a new micromobility option:

dockless bikes that didn't have to be returned to specific stations.

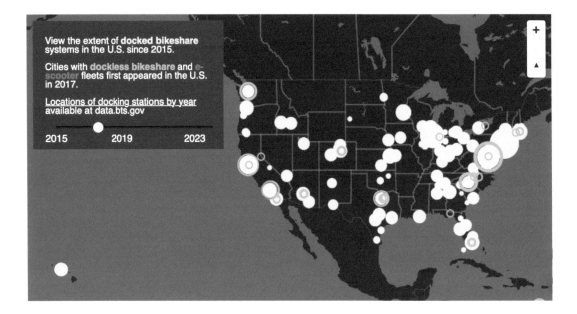

View the extent of **docked bikeshare** systems in the U.S. since 2015.

Cities with **dockless bikeshare** and **e-scooter** fleets first appeared in the U.S. in 2017.

Locations of docking stations by year available at data.bts.gov

2015   2019   2023

Above and opposite: Dockless bike-sharing and e-scooter systems first began to appear in the United States in 2017; by 2023, the country had 63 dockless bike-share systems and 252 e-scooter systems.

Previous: Testing out dockless bicycles in Beijing, China.

IMPLEMENTING A BIKE-SHARING SERVICE that has a real impact on city transportation usually means, among other things, getting the underlying system of docking stations right.

You'll need a "dense network of stations across the coverage area," advises the *Bike-Share Planning Guide,* published by the Institute for Transportation and Development Policy. "The utility of dock-based bike-sharing systems depends on the presence of a fairly continuous network of stations," agrees the Shared Mobility Toolkit, from the Shared-Use Mobility Center, "and building the network is a relatively capital- and labor-intensive task." The process also requires careful planning to make sure the stations are arranged in the most effective locations—and that they don't have negative side effects on their built environs.

But what if you could build a bike-share system with no stations at all, as some new enterprises in China are trying to do in a handful of major cities? One high-profile example is mobike, which launched in 2016 and already has a fleet in the tens of thousands in Beijing. Its chief executive is a veteran of Uber's operations in Shanghai, and it is backed by more than $100 million in investments from financial firms such as Sequoia Capital and Warburg Pincus.

Mobike's approach relies heavily on its unique smartphone app and technology built into the bike's patented design. Most significantly, the bikes don't need a docking station or even a parking dock. Instead, they are equipped with a special locking mechanism on the back wheel, meaning

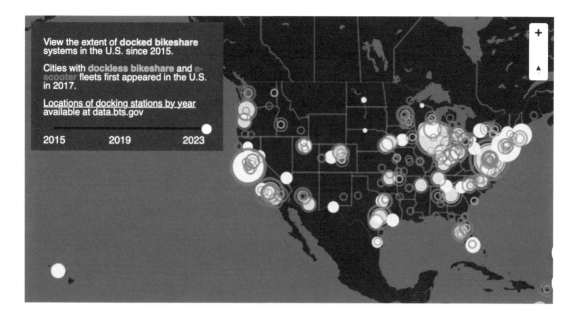

View the extent of **docked bikeshare** systems in the U.S. since 2015.

Cities with **dockless bikeshare** and e-scooter fleets first appeared in the U.S. in 2017.

Locations of docking stations by year available at data.bts.gov

2015   2019   2023

users can theoretically leave them almost anywhere except indoors and a few other locations. To locate an available bike, users consult the service's app, which presents a map that uses GPS technology to point out the nearest available mobikes; you can reserve one through the app to make sure nobody else snags it first. The app also generates a QR code that's used to unlock the bicycle.

The company is still too new to be fully proven, and it faces competition—including from another dock-free enterprise called ofo. But its stationless model may be as intriguing from a planning perspective as from a consumer's point of view.

Zhi Liu has tracked the development of bike-share programs in China for years. Formerly with the World Bank, where he focused in part on urban transportation issues, Liu is now director of the China program at the Lincoln Institute of Land Policy and the Peking University–Lincoln Institute Center for Urban Development and Land Policy in Beijing. He notes that it's important to understand the context in which these new businesses evolved.

China has a long history with cycling. But even for enthusiastic bike owners, rough and heavily trafficked roads make for a challenging long-distance commute in modern Chinese cities. So when bike-sharing schemes emerged in a few cities around 2008, as a complement to metro and bus options, the idea was quickly embraced. In 2011, the National Transport 12th Five Year Plan explicitly encouraged urban centers to develop bike-sharing as a useful addition to existing mass-transit systems.

Next: A dockless bike user pauses in Dongdan Street, Beijing, in 2017. When the systems were introduced, rental costs were often subsidized by investors to encourage widespread use. Riders paid about 14 US cents per hour.

Cities have experimented with public-private hybrid models, searching for a balance that would make bike-sharing cheap enough to attract users but profitable enough to cover costs.

"Planners and municipal governments now consider shared bikes a key component of public transport," Liu explains, "because it helps solve the problem of the so-called 'last mile.'" That is: you use public transport and arrive at a station—and you still have another mile to reach your real destination.

Government programs in China didn't face the same land use challenges that might arise in a US city, because urban land is state owned. But other challenges persisted. By 2011, when a World Bank conference focused on domestic and international experiences with shared bikes, the major discussion concerned "management and sustainability," Liu says. "What business model makes sense?"

A mix of solutions emerged. In Hangzhou, a government-led model involved setting up a state-owned company; today this is reportedly the largest bike-sharing system in the world. Other cities have experimented with various public-private hybrid models, searching for a balance that would make bike-sharing cheap enough to attract users but profitable enough to cover costs.

The latest wrinkle is businesses such as mobike and ofo, both of which also operate in other Chinese cities. These will clearly need to find that same economic equilibrium. But, perhaps because they're both lavishly funded, each seems more focused for the moment on building ridership and acceptance.

Ofo overtly targets students, using lighter bikes with combination locks, university-centric distribution, and a very low

A mobike tossed into the Thames in 2019. Mobike reported that 200,000 of its bicycles were lost to theft or vandalism that year. Since then, new geofencing technologies have improved the fate of dockless bikes.

deposit (13 yuan, or about $2). Mobike's target is more likely to be an urban professional and/or cycling enthusiast. The deposit is 299 yuan (a little less than $50); rental is 1 yuan per half-hour. Its cycles are heavier but also more durable and distinct. "I do hear a lot of people talking about it," says Hongye Fan, a Beijing-based consultant for the Asian Development Bank and investment manager for China Metro Corporation who has tracked bike-share programs. "It's an innovative model in China and spreading very fast."

Fan, previously an infrastructure finance and asset management consultant at the World Bank, points out some of the more intriguing side effects of the stationless models. Rolling out a major bike-sharing system can be, by necessity, a top-down process that doesn't leave much room for flexibility once dock locations are built out—or, she notes, for "really thinking about and analyzing: what is the real demand from the citizens?"

Instructions for renting an e-bike from Voi, a Swedish mobility company that provides dockless bicycles and scooters in more than 100 European cities.

Bike-sharing is a useful response to the last-mile problem, she continues, but "there is no universal last mile." In fact, a station fixed in a spot that's out of a particular user's way could turn the last mile into the last mile and a half. An almost Uber- or Zipcar-like system that's more overtly shaped by demand could avoid that.

And there are at least some experiments along similar lines elsewhere. A striking example is Copenhagen-based AirDonkey, essentially an app-based sharing platform that allows bike owners (including, notably, bike shops) to rent out their cycles to others. The startup hopes its model can work in other cities, even those where traditional share systems are in place.

The stationless model may be as intriguing from a planning perspective as from a consumer's point of view.

Of course, such approaches involve other challenges and hurdles. Theft has been an issue for mobike, as it would surely be in almost any city in the world, although the company has said it's a containable problem. Also, the demand-driven model could mean lots of bikes end up clustered in spots that are more popular as destinations than as starting points—meaning they'd have to be physically redistributed.

And, as Fan points out, planning would still play a crucial role in addressing problems that startups can't—like designing and ensuring proper infrastructure, such as bike lanes, that makes bike riding safe and practical. But that's true everywhere. Bike-share programs have proliferated wildly in recent years—Africa just launched its first, in Marrakech—and with an estimated 600 systems in place around the world, funding and implementation strategies vary. "We have not found any particular model that fits all cities," Liu says.

Truth is, we probably never will find a universal solution. And that's precisely why mobike and other new models—taking shape in China, the country with the most extensive bike-sharing systems anywhere—matter. Exploiting tech innovations in clever ways offers some compelling new potential routes to follow. Let's see whether others take these ideas for a spin and where that leads. ❯

Opposite: Riding an e-scooter in Castellón, Spain. Scooters now claim the largest portion of the global shared mobility market, constituting 42 percent of rides.

Below: Overcoming both criticism and logistical hurdles, dockless bike-sharing saw strong global growth in recent years.

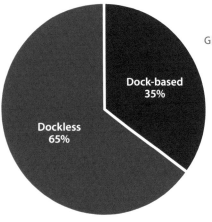

Dock-based
35%

Dockless
65%

Global Growth: New bike-sharing systems per type, launched 2021–2022

TYPE	NO. OF SYSTEMS
Dock-based	66
Dockless (Free-floating)	65
Dockless (Hubs/bays)	51
Dockless (Secure to street furniture)	2
Dockless (Hybrid—Docks and park-beside)	1
Dockless (Hybrid—Docks and hubs)	1
Dockless (Hybrid—Docks and free-float)	1
GRAND TOTAL	187

THE LATEST

The early enthusiasm for dockless bike-sharing (especially from investors) didn't take long to veer off course: bikes quickly began to clutter sidewalks, vacant lots, and waterways in cities around the world, and a vicious price war took a toll. By 2019, ofo had essentially ceased operation. Mobike fared better, remaining a market leader after Chinese online-services giant Meituan Dianping purchased it for $2.7 billion and renamed it Meituan Bike. With the help of improved technologies including geofencing—using location data to manage where a bike can be parked—dockless bike-sharing has bounced back, and thousands of bike and scooter systems now operate around the world. Dockless systems pioneered in China stand as an example of influential tech innovation shaping cities. "The extraordinarily rapid growth and destructive competition among bike-share firms that caused oversupply has ended, and the market appears much more orderly," says Zhi Liu, director of the China program at the Lincoln Institute of Land Policy. In cities like Beijing, Guangzhou, and Shenzhen, "some suppliers provide mopeds or e-bikes that have become more and more popular," he adds. "And cities have learned how to better manage bike-share parking spaces."

LEARN MORE   **Embracing the Improvisation of Dockless Bike-Share** (*Next City*)
https://nextcity.org/features/embracing-the-improvisation-of-dockless-bike-share

Bike-Share and E-Scooter Systems in the US (US Department of Transportation)
https://data.bts.gov/stories/s/Bikeshare-and-e-scooters-in-the-U-S-/fwcs-jprj

Understanding the Rise of Tech in China (*Harvard Business Review*)
https://hbr.org/2022/09/understanding-the-rise-of-tech-in-china

WHY PLANNERS WANT YOUR (ANONYMIZED) APP DATA

An estimated 85 percent of Americans now carry smartphones capable of tracking their location.

This data, properly anonymized, can be invaluable to the private sector and to planners and other public policymakers—for studying traffic patterns and mobility, shaping transportation strategies, and more.

Above: Data from athletic apps can generate real-world insights for planners and other municipal officials.

Previous: Pedestrians in Birmingham, England.

FOUNDED IN 2009 as a "social network for athletes," San Francisco–based Strava is today best known for its popular smartphone app, used by millions of people all over the world to track and share their biking, running, and walking activity. Some users are serious athletes, but plenty simply track commutes or routine exercise excursions as part of a basic fitness regimen. As a result, Strava has built up a massive dataset showing how bikers and pedestrians move through cities. And a couple of years ago, the company decided to do something with this information—"to give back to the people on Strava," says Brian Devaney, the marketing lead for Strava Metro.

On its site, the company released a global "heat map": a visual and inter-active presentation of its (anonymized) data. You could zoom in on, say, a San Francisco neighborhood to see which routes Strava users travel most frequently. Customers seemed to enjoy this. But the company also heard from another audience that it hadn't counted on. "We started to get all these emails from city planning groups and departments of transportation," Devaney explains. They wanted access to Strava's data, which many recog-nized as potentially useful for planning both short- and long-range transpor-tation and infrastructure projects, or for tracking and demonstrating actual usage and behavior of completed projects.

This was "completely unexpected," Devaney continues, but the company has embraced the development. It formed its new Strava Metro division specifically to help municipalities get the most out of its data. "That was never on a product roadmap or any Strava long-term strategic plan," Devaney says. "It just sort of happened."

It's also one example of a promising convergence of planners' appetite for an emerging category of data—and a perhaps surprising willingness of for-profit businesses to feed that appetite. Another example is Waze, the map and directions app that relies in part on user-submitted information about traffic conditions to suggest the best driving route between two points in real time. (Waze is now owned by Google, which incorporates some of its data into Google Maps, but remains a stand-alone app.)

A couple of years ago, Waze launched its Connected Citizens Program, easing two-way data sharing between its users and various municipal entities. Apart from allowing cities to in effect communicate road closures and other projects to users in real time, the program also helps inform potential planning decisions by revealing locations with frequent traffic

Apart from allowing cities to communicate road closures and other projects to users in real time, the program also helps inform potential planning decisions by revealing locations with frequent traffic congestion or other problems.

congestion or other problems. Last year, Waze partnered with Esri, which makes digital-mapping software for cities. The goal is to use data that Waze generates about traffic patterns to help guide transportation planning—and to reduce reliance on much more expensive data-collection methods involving internet-connected sensors and the like.

Most recently, the ride-sharing company Uber has launched Uber Movement, a service that provides planners and researchers information about travel times, road conditions, and other data, culled from the billions of rides the company's drivers have made. "We don't manage streets. We don't plan infrastructure," Andrew Salzberg, Uber's chief of transportation policy, told *Wired* magazine. "So why have this stuff bottled up when it can provide immense value to the cities we're working in?"

Taken together, such efforts present some fresh opportunities—and some interesting new challenges—for transportation planning. "It's a big leap in terms of quantity of data," says Julie Campoli, founder of the Burlington-based practice Terra Firma Urban Design and author of *Made for Walking: Density and Neighborhood Form,* published by the

Next: LA County Parks has used anonymized data from fitness apps to better understand how people use public space and to inform investments in facilities in underserved neighborhoods, such as the Earvin "Magic" Johnson Recreation Area.

Below: Officials examine Waze data at the Transportation Department in Medellín, Colombia, one of the cities that has partnered with the app to improve infrastructure planning (an alliance touted by the sign).

Anonymized activity data helped officials in Queensland, Australia, confirm that public demand for the New Farm Riverwalk justified the cost of rebuilding it.

Lincoln Institute of Land Policy. And on one level, this can be more informative than travel survey data gathered in an expensive and time-consuming process involving detailed questions about transit behavior.

But as rich as the newer data may be, it can carry biases: any given app's user base may have demographic skews. And, as Campoli points out, not everyone has a smartphone. "It's great to have that information," she says. "But it's important to remember that it doesn't represent everyone."

A closer look at how Strava Metro data has been put to real-world use shows how these massive new caches of information can be thoughtfully integrated into existing processes. Data analysts in the Department of Transport and Main Roads (TMR) in Queensland, Australia, took an early interest in Strava's data. Michael Langdon, a senior advisor in the TMR with a focus on cycling and walking, explains that the department had already been gathering and making use of global positioning system (GPS) data for years, but it was a cumbersome process involving lots of dedicated GPS units and relying on subjects to use them regularly and properly. "When we saw Strava, what hit us was: this actually automates a lot of the processes that we had to do manually," Langdon says.

Devaney of Strava explains that, as a private entity focused on building its user base and business, the company hadn't been collecting, storing, or

Just because citizens say they'd like a new bike pathway doesn't mean they'll use it. This time, the department had hard data to demonstrate impressive usage levels.

packaging its data with municipal planning uses in mind. So it had to devote research and development efforts into making the material easily usable by cities (learning to extract the relevant details, and making them compatible with widely used software and systems), and building out a team to work specifically with planning professionals. Beta partnerships with Portland, Oregon, and Orlando, Florida, honed the process, and by the end of 2016 Strava Metro was working with more than 100 municipalities. It charges annual usage fees to cover costs; these vary depending on details.

Queensland was another early partner. Mindful of precisely the sorts of biases and limitations Campoli cites, and other potential flaws, its TMR set about "analyzing and calibrating" Strava's data, ultimately publishing a detailed study of its assessment. In short, the research concluded that smartphone GPS data is best in conjunction with other data sources but can be particularly useful in evaluating the impact of a specific infrastructure project.

A GPS heat map generated in Portland, Oregon, shows one person's walking routes over time. Similar maps using aggregated data can give planners a better understanding of the non-motorized travel routes of residents and visitors.

In fact, the department has successfully used Strava data in precisely that manner. One example involved the replacement of a floating bike-and-walk pathway destroyed in a 2011 Brisbane River flood. It took several years for officials to commit to rebuilding the New Farm Riverwalk, and the TMR sought to demonstrate that the new structure was really having an impact. "People question: 'Why are we building this? Are people even going to use this? I've never seen a cyclist on that road or bridge'," Langdon says, referring to transportation infrastructure projects in general. Traditional surveys don't necessarily answer those questions in an empirical way: just because citizens say they'd like a new bike pathway doesn't mean they'll use it.

This time, the TMR had hard information to demonstrate impressive usage levels and to detail the impact on cycling behavior on surrounding roads and routes. "The Strava data does allow us to prove what actually happened," Langdon says.

And that, in turn, helps new planning initiatives. Langdon points to another example involving the creation of new bikeways along a major motorway. Like many big investments, it has rolled out in stages. Analysis of an early phase, using Strava data cross-referenced with official crash data and other sources, showed a 12 percent increase in bike usage over the prior bikeway—as well as a notable deflection of cyclists away from a nearby, car-trafficked road where accidents were common. "That helped us argue: 'this is why we need to complete the other sections,' because we were already seeing this benefit," he says.

The upshot, Langdon concludes, is that having calibrated and learned to use what Strava Metro offers, it's evolved into a regular part of the department's planning toolkit: "it's become pretty stock-standard for us now."

Strava Metro points to other examples in Seattle, Glasgow, London, and elsewhere. The payoff for the company, Devaney says, is that enhanced cycling and pedestrian infrastructure indirectly help encourage the behaviors at the core of its current and potential future user base. For other firms, motives may differ. For example, Waze's end-user experience is directly improved by two-way communication with cities; Uber wants to position itself as more of a partner to municipalities; and so on.

Clearly incorporating such data streams into planning practices takes effort, on both sides. But even if makers of popular apps that rely in part on corralling behavioral data never considered how cities and planners could use that information, it's encouraging that some are taking thoughtful approaches to that possibility. And the same goes for cities looking for fresh insights to guide decisions. As Campoli observes: "it's another piece of a puzzle." ›

Above: Fitness app data helped determine where demand for new bicycle infrastructure was highest in Catalonia, Spain.

Opposite: The City of Atlanta Department of Transportation has used Strava Metro data to inform projects including Vision Zero, an initiative designed to rework streets and minimize traffic fatalities.

WHY PLANNERS WANT YOUR (ANONYMIZED) APP DATA

THE LATEST

Strava, the popular exercise app, was an early example of a company figuring out how to make its data available for and useful to cities and municipalities. Strava Metro, a spin-off data platform that allows partner organizations access to de-identified data to aid transportation planners, recently marked its 10th anniversary and has helped shape projects from Atlanta to Los Angeles County, Paris to Catalonia. More recently, the company has added potential carbon-saving data to commuter-tracked activity it measures. Other data sources, such as Placer.ai—an analytics platform that launched in late 2018 and had secured $100 million in funding by early 2022—have also begun working with cities as well as business clients. Concerns over potential privacy pitfalls remain, and the data presents only a limited picture. But data culled from apps and technologies that have little to do with planning has become an increasingly common tool available to shape city development and land use.

LEARN MORE

Sustainable Cities, One Stride at a Time (Harvard Kennedy School)
https://datasmart.hks.harvard.edu/sustainable-cities-one-stride-time

How Cellphone and Fitness App Data Is Helping Create Equity in Public Parks
(American Planning Association)
https://www.planning.org/planning/2023/summer/
how-cellphone-and-fitness-app-data-is-helping-create-equity-in-public-parks

Smart Growth Loves Heatmaps (*Planetizen*)
https://www.planetizen.com/blogs/114678-smart-growth-loves-heatmaps

QUANTIFYING THE ECONOMIC BENEFIT OF TREES

Cities lose millions of trees a year to new development and other factors.

One response has been to reconceptualize trees as an element of vital green infrastructure— harnessing and organizing data to make clear the economic benefits of a robust urban canopy, and the true costs of a shrinking one.

Above: A student in Bangladesh with a tree that she and her classmates tagged using i-Tree. The tag identifies the tree species and the monetary value of the benefits it will provide— from shade to carbon sequestration— over the next 20 years.

Previous: A tree grows in Dusseldorf.

A 2012 UNITED STATES FOREST SERVICE STUDY of urban tree cover estimated that American cities were losing around four million trees per year. Worldwide, agriculture, logging, and other factors eliminate 18.7 million acres of forest annually, according to the World Wildlife Fund. Yet the cost of that loss is hard to quantify. It's widely recognized that plants absorb carbon dioxide, helping to mitigate the effects of climate change, but city planners could benefit from a more precise, data-driven assessment of the urban canopy's value to guide how trees and other vegetation can most sensibly figure into the design and planning of the contemporary city.

After all, that's how we evaluate and install gray infrastructure, counting every light pole and parking lot to help us think about how these elements work in a city's design. Historically, we haven't been as thoughtful or demanding about quantifying, and thus managing, green infrastructure, according to David Nowak, a senior scientist with the US Forest Service.

As a rule, cities compile and track the details of the built infrastructure, but not trees. This makes it harder to plan for, or even debate, the various potential impacts of maintaining, increasing, or reducing urban vegetation.

But that has been changing. Nowak leads a pioneering Forest Service project called i-Tree, a suite of Web tools drawing in part on geographic information system (GIS) data. I-Tree combines satellite imagery and other

As a rule, cities compile and track the details of the built infrastructure, but not trees. This makes it harder to plan for, or even debate, the various potential impacts of maintaining, increasing, or reducing urban vegetation.

data to help citizens, researchers, and officials understand urban canopies and other green infrastructure elements, often in economic terms.

For example, an i-Tree analysis of Austin, Texas, found that trees save the city about $19 million a year in residential energy use, $11.6 million in carbon capture, and almost $3 million in pollution removal. The city's arboreal infrastructure produces oxygen and consumes carbon dioxide, for instance, adding up to a reduction in carbon emissions that i-Tree values at $5 million annually. Other tree payoffs—some quantified, others not—include absorbing ultraviolet radiation, helping absorb rainwater, and reducing noise pollution.

In another i-Tree analysis, conducted in 2017, researchers in the United States and Italy concluded that, worldwide, cities with populations over 10 million realize median annual savings of $505 million from reduced air pollution, mitigated heat island effects, and other benefits derived from their urban canopies.

This type of analysis can help cities deploy green resources for maximum impact and understand the tradeoffs involved in many planning decisions. Clearing trees to make way for a parking lot entails a loss, not just the gain associated with increased parking, Nowak noted.

In the past, trees were more likely a concern for the parks or forestry department. Increasingly, they're central to cities' responses to climate change. "I can tell you definitively that cities and towns across the nation are very interested in figuring out, whether or not you can talk about climate change politically, 'What exactly are we going to do about it today?'," said Jim Levitt, director of land conservation programs at the Lincoln Institute of Land Policy, and director of conservation

Next: San Francisco's densely developed Mission District boasts 6,859 trees in public spaces, or about one for every seven people.

Below: The Ithaca Commons, a four-block pedestrian shopping area in downtown Ithaca, New York, is planted with local species of trees, shrubs, perennials, and annuals.

An i-Tree analysis of Austin, Texas, found that trees save the city about $19 million a year in residential energy use, $11.6 million in carbon capture, and almost $3 million in pollution removal.

innovation at the Harvard Forest. That's true from New England to Miami to Newport News, Virginia, and Phoenix, he added, even if the specific reasons vary, whether flood issues, heat island effects, or others.

Recent arboreal infrastructure-related technology responds directly to this city-level interest. In late 2016, MIT's Senseable City Lab, in collaboration with the World Economic Forum, launched a tool called Treepedia and has since published analyses of tree coverage in 27 cities around the world. In an interesting twist, it draws not on the satellite data behind many GIS projects, but on imagery culled from Google Street View. It offers a different skew on tree data, since, for example, it underrepresents large urban parks. But this is by design. The tool's creators believe that detailing the "street greenery" citizens actually experience can inform the planning process. The lab will continue to add cities and has a backlog of

Treepedia, a project developed by the MIT Senseable City Lab, used Google Street View to calculate a Green View Index for cities around the world.

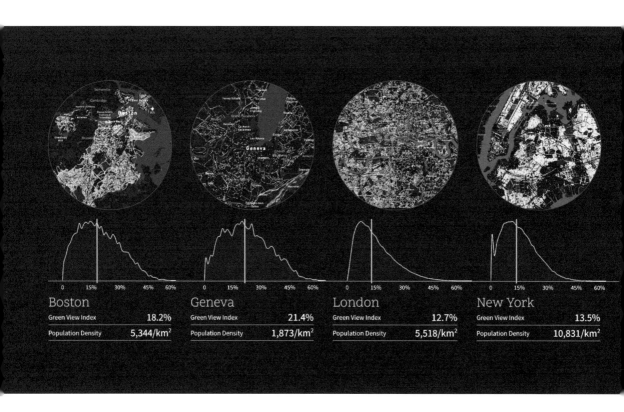

Boston		Geneva		London		New York	
Green View Index	18.2%	Green View Index	21.4%	Green View Index	12.7%	Green View Index	13.5%
Population Density	5,344/km²	Population Density	1,873/km²	Population Density	5,518/km²	Population Density	10,831/km²

QUANTIFYING THE ECONOMIC BENEFIT OF TREES

L'arbre des philatélistes à La Haye

Absorption d'eau
5.700 litres par an

Surface de la couronne **380 m²**

Couverture de couronne dans
un quartier résidentiel qui passe de 10 à 25 %
= baisse de la température de **2°C**

PASSEPORT I-TREE ECO

	Lieu La Haye, Palais Noordeinde
	Nom Arbre des philatélistes
Espèce	
Marronnier d'Inde (*Aesculus hippocastanum* 'Baumannii')	
Diamètre couronne 23 m	Âge 138 ans
Diamètre tronc 107 cm	Hauteur 17,4 m

Superficie foliaire 1.532 m²
= **1,7** millions de
timbres postes

Fixation de CO₂
45,5 kg/an =
émission d'un trajet
de 425 km en voiture

Filtre par an
1,6 kg
de substances
polluantes
dans l'air

Diamètre du tronc
= **169** arbres
d'un diamètre de 4 cm

L'arbre des philatélistes se trouve à La Haye, devant le Palais de Noordeinde. Il doit son nom au fait que pendant de nombreuses années des timbres-poste s'échangeaient et se vendaient sous l'arbre et tout autour de celui-ci.

Avantages écologiques de l'arbre des philatélistes :
• Absorption d'eau € 6,50 par an.
• Captage de pollution de l'air €111 par an.
• Fixation du CO₂ € 16 par an.
• Stockage de CO₂ € 1.407.

requests from municipalities, academics, and others, according to Carlo Ratti, director of the MIT Senseable City Lab and founder of the design firm Carlo Ratti Associati.

"Cities are trying to acquire better information and understand the current state of the urban canopy," Ratti said. "Most of them do not have the resources to manually survey the entire city. Treepedia data can give them a solid baseline" and focus efforts where they may be needed most. "Others, like planners and designers, find it useful as a proxy for measuring the perception of green space and trees by citizens," he said, because it captures a kind of shared perspective "from the ground." The lab will soon release an open-source version of its software to let cities, nongovernmental organizations, and community groups compile their own data. The hope is that NGOs and local groups will use Treepedia "as a tool to both determine where planting is needed and lobby their local governments with evidence-based campaigns," Ratti explained.

This is consistent with a broader interest among citizens and planners in green city initiatives, including high-profile projects from New York to Atlanta and beyond. Nowak, of the i-Tree program, said that its tools helped guide the organizers of Million Trees NYC, a public-private initiative that

An infographic touting the benefits of trees at the Hague's Palais Noordeinde illustrates the global reach of the i-Tree tool.

> "We want to help answer the question: If I can plant only
> one tree or make one change to the city's green landscape,
> where should I do it?"

increased New York's aggregate urban forest by an estimated 20 percent. The London i-Tree Eco Project, according to its 2015 report, used i-Tree to quantify "the structure of the urban forest (the physical attributes such as tree density, tree health, leaf area, and biomass)," with a specific eye toward capturing its value "in monetary terms." Carbon sequestration savings logged in at £4.79 million (roughly $6.75 million) annually, according to the report. "Our hope is to provide numbers that are locally derived, to help people make informed decisions—whether it's pro or against trees," Nowak said.

One i-Tree web application, Landscape, is intended for planners in particular. Users can explore tree canopy, cross-matched with basic demographic information down to the census-block level, offering data related to pollution mitigation, temperature impacts, and other factors. For example, users can easily identify areas with high population density but low tree cover. The i-Tree project is adding data on tree species over the next year and is seeking feedback to modify the tool in ways that make the most sense for planning, according to Nowak.

The broad idea is the same one that has shaped i-Tree from the start—a data-driven approach to thinking about green infrastructure. "We want to help answer the question: If I can plant only one tree or make one change to the city's green landscape, where should I do it?" Nowak said. ❯

Opposite: A community tree planting in Washington, DC, with local urban forestry nonprofit Casey Trees. New apps are helping officials and residents track the health and maintenance of urban trees in DC and other cities.

Below: An i-Tree analysis shows forest types in Utah, Wyoming, and Colorado.

QUANTIFYING THE ECONOMIC BENEFIT OF TREES

THE LATEST

The effort to quantify the economic benefit of trees has inspired ambitious projects to help city planners and policymakers catalog, and make decisions about, green infrastructure. MIT's Senseable City Lab released an open-source Python library for its Treepedia tool, which 34 cities have now used to catalog their street greenery; unfortunately, the Google Street View imagery the tool relies on is no longer freely available, making it prohibitively expensive for new cities to take part. The Forest Service, however, continues to add to its suite of canopy-measuring i-Tree tools and hosts regular virtual i-Tree Academy seminars for new and existing users. Meanwhile, new tactics and tools have emerged to grow citizen engagement with urban trees, including interactive digital maps that allow residents to help maintain and track the health of trees in their communities, from Berlin's *Gieß den Kiez* (Water the Neighborhood) to the NYC Tree Map, the most comprehensive living-tree map in the world.

LEARN MORE **i-Tree** (US Forest Service)
https://www.itreetools.org

Treepedia (MIT Senseable City Lab)
https://senseable.mit.edu/treepedia

City Tech: Tree-Watering Apps for the Urban Forest (Lincoln Institute of Land Policy)
https://www.lincolninst.edu/publications/articles/2023-08-city-tech-tree-watering-apps-urban-forests-berlin-athens-dc-new-york

PRINTABLE BUILDINGS TAKE SHAPE

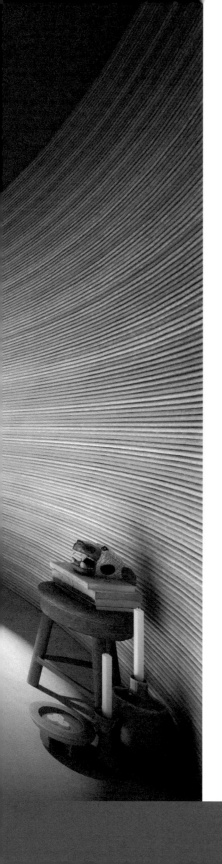

Just a few years ago, 3D printing an entire building sounded like an exotic experiment, or maybe a stunt.

Today, while far from routine, this high-tech construction process is more popular than ever— and becoming a reality in cities around the world.

Above: A rendering of the world's first habitable 3D-printed homes in Eindhoven, the Netherlands. The first residents moved into a single-story home in the development in 2021. Construction on four additional homes is expected to begin in 2025.

Previous: Plans for El Cosmico, the world's first 3D-printed hotel, currently in development in Marfa, Texas.

OVER THE PAST DECADE, three-dimensional printing has been one of the buzziest ideas in technology. Instead of adding ink to paper, a 3D printer translates a digital design into an object by adding layer upon layer of material (plastic, metal, concrete) through a computer-guided extruder—almost like a motorized toothpaste tube. More correctly but blandly described as "additive manufacturing," the process has evolved from rapid-prototyping uses by tech corporations and design firms to widespread experimentation by hobbyists and hackers and startups as they make objects from consumer products to toys.

But what about something bigger—like a house?

Actually, for several years, researchers and entrepreneurs around the world have been applying variations of the technique to increasingly ambitious building-sized projects. The latest example involves a five-house development in Eindhoven, the Netherlands. It's an ambitious experiment involving multiple partners that will wrestle with not only the practicalities of design and construction, but also regulations and the real-world marketplace, given that the properties are rentals. "We need a big revolution in the building industry," said Rudy van Gurp, the project manager for building contractor Van Wijnen Rosmalen. The application of 3D-printing techniques could be part of that.

"We need a big revolution in the building industry."

The advantages of this still-evolving form of building include more efficient use of materials, which cuts costs and minimizes waste; speed of construction; and potential for customization. Or at least that's the promise, if the technology continues to improve at its current pace. That's one reason the Eindhoven experiment is notable, as it follows a recent burst of related prototyping breakthroughs.

In 2017 a firm called ICON in Austin, Texas, used its 3D-printing technology to build a sleek, intentionally minimalist 350-square-foot home for a reported $10,000, predicting it could knock the cost down to $4,000 as it modifies its design to further reduce nonprinted elements. The structure was built to meet local housing codes and is being used as a model home and office. Envisioning the process as a potential solution to housing needs

As 3D-printing techniques evolve, building two-story homes like this one in Houston is becoming a viable option, opening up the possibility for multifamily housing.

What will matter in the longer run is how the technology gets merged into existing city planning objectives, as well as broader thinking about development and land use.

in the developing world, ICON is working with the nonprofit New Story to bring its approach to El Salvador.

And in July, a French family of five was chosen to be the first in the world to actually move into a 3D-printed house: a detached, 1,000-square-foot social housing unit with eye-catching curves. The organizers of that project say it cost about $200,000, which they say is 20 percent less than an identical version built using traditional methods. The structure took 54 hours to print—although it took another four months to finish nonprinted elements such as the windows and roof.

ICON's Vulcan construction system weighs 9,500 pounds. It can print five to 10 inches of Lavacrete, the company's proprietary material, each second.

Build time and cost are both projected to fall as the process is refined. But what will matter in the longer run is how the technology gets merged into existing city planning objectives, as well as broader thinking about

development and land use. That's the other reason the Eindhoven project is compelling: one of the various parties looking to explore, and influence, the future of construction there is the city itself.

"I was wondering why [construction] was such a traditional sector," Vice Mayor Yasin Torunoglu reflected. "It has always been the same way of building houses and new buildings." And that has led to practical and workaday problems. For instance, the Netherlands has a shortage of skilled bricklayers, which seems like a very 20th-century reason for a construction delay. "I was wondering where the [tech] revolution was," Torunoglu said.

In helping coordinate the partnership behind what is now called Project Milestone, Torunoglu wanted the city to be directly involved in shaping technology's impact and regulatory implications—not trailing behind and reacting to change created by others, as is so often the case with tech disruption.

Other partners in the effort include the Eindhoven University of Technology and the design firm Houben en Van Mierlo Architecten. The core technology, developed by the university, was used to build the world's first concrete 3D-printed bridge in 2017. A big mechanical nozzle mounted on a frame squeezes concrete in precise amounts in a programmed pattern—building walls and forms as a 3D printer would, but on a larger scale.

The latest effort will play out over five years and, like 3D printing itself, will build up layer by layer. The first house is a one-story, two-bedroom

Above: Habitat for Humanity built this 3D-printed home in Williamsburg, Virginia, with Colorado-based company Alquist. Housing advocates believe the technology could offer a promising solution to the global affordability crisis.

Next: On-site printers can build the exterior walls of a home in 20 to 30 hours, reducing the time needed for conventional framing by three to six weeks.

structure. It will be built largely in the university's construction lab and transported and assembled on-site. (Plumbing and wiring are accommodated in the printed designs and finished on-site.) The subsequent houses are steadily larger and more ambitious. The team will draw lessons from each construction to shape the next, on everything from building details to coding issues. The final structure will be printed on-site.

The designs are striking, idiosyncratic, and almost blobby, with distinct and unpredictable curves. This is a direct result of the 3D-printing process. Designs can be tweaked and modified house by house in a way that allows "true mass customization," builder van Gurp said: "Every house can have a different look." Torunoglu, the Eindhoven vice mayor, made a similar point, arguing that the process could "democratize the industry," offering homebuyers unprecedented design input.

Opposite: A 3D printer lays specialized concrete using, yes, a 3D-printed nozzle.

Below: Homes under construction at Wolf Ranch, a development of 100 3D-printed houses by ICON in Georgetown, Texas.

PRINTABLE BUILDINGS TAKE SHAPE

If promised improvements materialize, this method would be up to 40 percent cheaper than standard construction, advocates of the burgeoning industry say.

Of course, that's a long way off. The process is "really interesting and could reduce the cost of housing in a significant way," says Armando Carbonell, former senior fellow and urban form expert at the Lincoln Institute of Land Policy. "But that's a 'could.'"

If promised improvements materialize, this method would be up to 40 percent cheaper than standard construction, advocates of the burgeoning industry say. But as significant as that would be, the impact would still vary. In hot markets like New York or San Francisco, the portion of housing costs attributable to land value is two or three times construction costs (meaning houses cost a lot because of where they're located, not how they're built); this method would be more effective in those cities if it proves possible to build up, increasing density. In cooler markets like Cleveland or St. Louis, where construction drives the cost of housing, 3D-printed homes could drastically lower such costs, Carbonell says. This could have an even greater impact in developing-world contexts.

The Eindhoven project is directed at higher-end consumers, but that could still significantly help establish 3D printing as a viable construction option, because its success or failure depends on actual market acceptance. "It's a challenge to learn from this process," Eindhoven Vice Mayor Torunoglu said. "We have to collaborate with the market."

In a good sign for that collaboration, more than 100 people have already signed up as potential renters. That level of interest isn't something you can manufacture. ❯

Opposite: Habitat for Humanity homeowners learn how to use the 3D printer provided with their new house.

Below: Employees of Alquist. The company's name refers to a character in a satirical 1920 play who believed humans and robots could peacefully coexist.

THE LATEST

The occupants of the first structure in the 3D-printed, five-home "Milestone Project" in Eindhoven, the Netherlands, moved in during spring 2021. Meanwhile, the trend has rapidly spread: pioneering Texas construction technology firm ICON is developing a neighborhood of 100 energy-efficient homes north of Austin, has used the technology to build affordable homes in Mexico and Texas, and is working on robotic and AI technologies designed to help "tackle the global housing crisis and prepare to build on other worlds." Habitat for Humanity, working with construction partners Alquist and the PERI Group, unveiled its first 3D-printed homes in Williamsburg, Virginia, and Tempe, Arizona, in 2022. Advocates increasingly tout the technology's possible role in addressing the affordable housing crisis, in both the United States and developing countries. That promise would require a significant scaling up of the industry, but the proof of concept looks a lot sturdier than it did a few years ago.

LEARN MORE **3D-Printed Housing Milestone in Houston Bodes Well for Future of Affordable Construction** (Urban Land Institute)
https://urbanland.uli.org/public/3d-printed-housing-milestone-in-houston-bodes-well-for-future-of-affordable-housing

Project Milestone: Eindhoven
https://www.3dprintedhouse.nl/en/project-info/project-milestone

Live Life in 3D (Habitat for Humanity)
https://habitatpgw.org/3d

PRECISION MAPPING WATER IN THE DESERT

Thirsty for details about local vulnerability to heat, flooding, and other climate impacts, several Southwest communities embarked on an ambitious mapping effort.

The project helped them see their landscapes in a whole new light.

Above: In Tucson, Arizona, officials have used cutting-edge mapping technology to better understand flooding and climate-related risks.

Previous: The bed of the Santa Cruz River in Tucson.

THE DESERT CITY OF TUCSON, ARIZONA, has an average annual rainfall of just 12 inches. But when the rain comes, it often comes in the form of torrential downpours, causing damaging floods across the city. This is an ironic challenge for Tucson and the broader Pima County area in which it is situated, given that it's part of a much larger region working to ensure that there is—and will continue to be—enough water to go around in a time of unrelenting drought.

Both of these distinct water-management challenges—too dry and too wet—can be addressed by thoughtful land use and infrastructure decisions. Of course, when making such decisions, it helps to have precise mapping data on hand. That's why Pima County officials are working with the Lincoln Institute's Babbitt Center for Land and Water Policy and other key partners to pilot the use of some of the most cutting-edge mapping and data analysis tools on the market.

For the Babbitt Center—founded in 2017 with the mission of providing water and land use research and education to communities throughout the Colorado River Basin—the partnership represents one early step in exploring how such technology can be used to help integrate water and land use management across the region.

PRECISION MAPPING WATER IN THE DESERT

The technology can now provide resolution that makes observing and classifying land in one-square-meter chunks possible, while 30 square meters was the limit previously.

The technology itself originated across the country, at the Conservation Innovation Center (CIC) of Maryland's Chesapeake Conservancy, a key player in cleaning up the notoriously pollution-addled Chesapeake Bay. To oversimplify a bit: CIC has designed image analysis algorithms that provide distinctly more granular image data of the Earth's surface. The technology can now provide resolution that makes observing and classifying land in one-square-meter chunks possible, while 30 square meters was the limit previously.

The details are of course a little more complicated, explains Jeff Allenby, the CIC's former director of conservation technology. Allenby says the new technology addresses a historic challenge: the compromise between resolution and cost of image collection. Until relatively recently, you could get 30-meter data collected via satellite every couple of weeks or even days. Or you could get more granular data collected via airplane—but at such a high cost that it was only worth doing every few years at most, which meant it was less timely.

What's changing, says Allenby, is both the camera technology and the nature of the satellites used to deploy it. Instead of launching a super-expensive satellite built to last for decades, newer companies the CIC works with—Allenby mentions Planet Labs and DigitalGlobe—are using different approaches. "Smaller, replaceable" satellites, meant to

Next: Precision maps created by Planet Labs in 2020 show the Green River in Utah during four seasons (clockwise from top left): winter, spring, summer, and fall.

Below: Chesapeake Conservancy geospatial project manager Rachel Soobitsky reviews detailed land cover data from Tucson in 2019. Soobitsky now works at NASA.

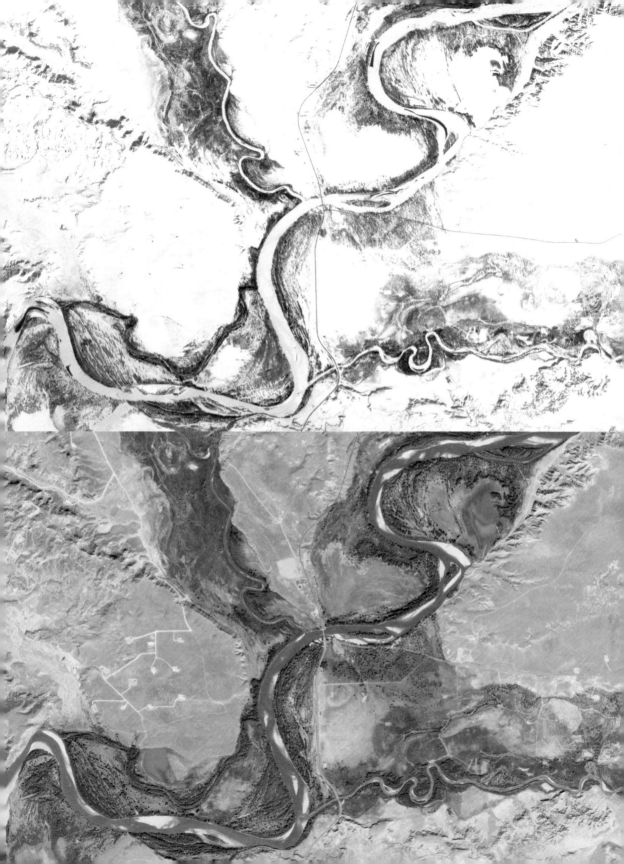

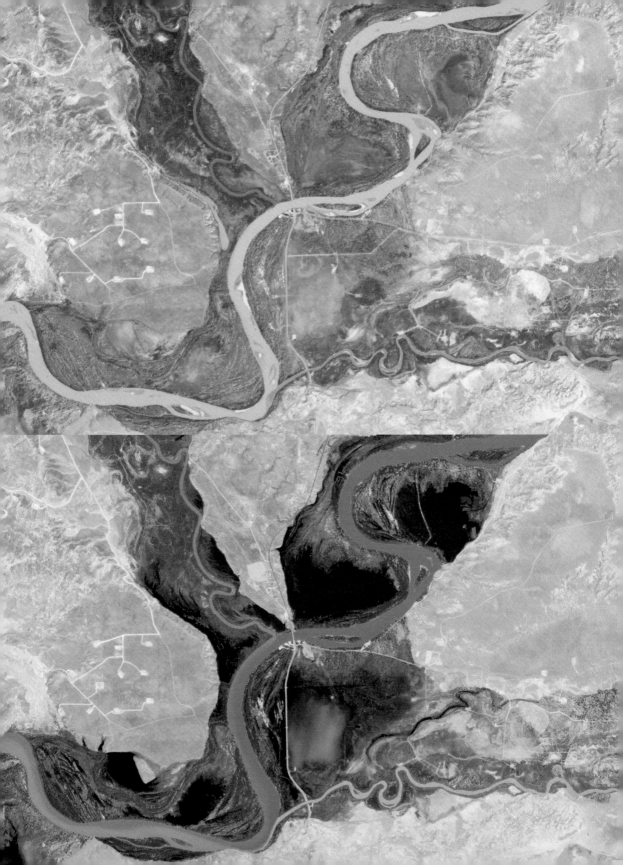

Team members at Planet Labs monitor satellites from the company's "mission control" room in 2017.

last just a couple of years before they burn off in the atmosphere, can be equipped with the latest camera technology. Deployed in a kind of network, they offer coverage of most of the planet, producing new image data almost constantly.

Technology companies developed this business model to respond to commercial and investor demand for the most recent information available; tracking the number of cars in big-box store parking lots can, in theory, be a valuable economic indicator. Land use planners don't need images quite that close to real time. But Allenby says the CIC began asking the tech companies, "What are you doing with the imagery that's two weeks old?" It's less expensive to acquire, but far better than what was previously available.

The resulting images are interpreted by computers that classify them by type: irrigated land, bedrock, grassland, and so on. Doing that at a 30-square-meter level required a lot of compromise and imprecision; the one-meter level is a different story.

An overview of the LiDAR (Light Detection and Ranging) elevation data collection process.

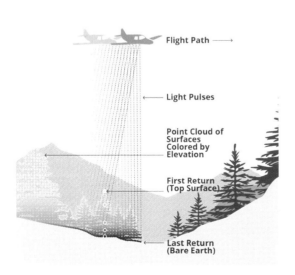

Flight Path ——→

←—— Light Pulses

Point Cloud of
Surfaces
Colored by
Elevation

First Return
(Top Surface)

Last Return
(Bare Earth)

The goal is to "model how water moves across a landscape," as Allenby puts it, by combining the data with other resources, most notably LiDAR (Light Detection and Ranging) elevation data. Those are the "flour and eggs" of land use data projects, supplemented with other ingredients like reduction efficiencies or load rates from different land cover, depending on the project, Allenby says: "We're building new recipes." For Chesapeake Bay, those recipes are meant to help manage water quality. If you can determine where water is concentrating and, say, taking on nitrogen, you can deduce the most cost-effective spot to plant trees or place a riparian buffer to reduce that nitrogen load.

In the Colorado River Basin, the most urgent current water-management challenges are about quantity. Since water policy is largely hashed out at the local level despite the underlying land use issues having implications across multiple states, the Babbitt Center serves as a resource across a broad region. There's currently a "heightened awareness" of water management among municipal and county policymakers, says Paula Randolph, the Babbitt Center's former associate director. "People are wanting to think about these issues and realizing they don't have enough information."

That brings us back to Pima County. Although it lies outside the basin, it boasts two features that make it a good place to evaluate how the uses of precision mapping data might be applied in the West: basin-like geography and proactive municipal leaders. When the manager of technology for the Pima Association of Governments saw Allenby speak about the benefits of his work in the East, he contacted the CIC to discuss possibilities for the West. A year into the resulting project, several partners were on board, the group was mapping a 3,800-square-mile area, and the open-source data lived on the Pima Regional Flood Control District website, where others throughout the county could access and use it.

Broadly, this process has taken some effort, Randolph notes. Satellite data gathered in the West has different contours than the East Coast imagery that Chesapeake's sophisticated software was used to, and that has required some adjustment—"teaching" the software the difference between a Southwestern rock roof and a front yard that both look (to the machine) like dirt, for instance. "We need human partners to fix that," she says. "We strive for management-quality decision-making data."

Even as such refinements continue, there are already

The Chesapeake Conservancy used satellite data to help Pima County, Arizona, officials better understand evapotranspiration, or the amount of water entering the atmosphere from plants or surface water.

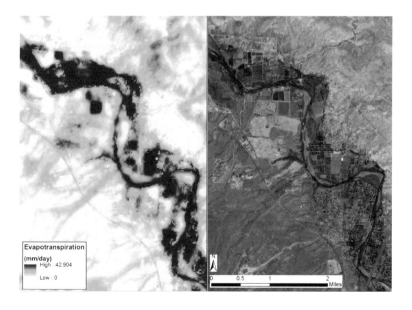

Evapotranspiration (mm/day)
High : 42.904
Low : 0

0   0.5   1   2 Miles

N

The hope is that the results will contribute to a global conversation around water-management experimentation.

some early results in Pima County. Clearer and more precise data about land cover is helping to identify areas that need flood mitigation. It has also been useful in identifying "hot spots" where dangerous heat island effects can occur, offering guidance for mitigation actions like adding shade trees. These maps provide a visual showcase about water flow and land use more efficiently than a field worker could.

Both Allenby and Randolph stress that this partnership is still in the early phases of exploring the potential uses and impacts of high-resolution map data. Randolph points out that while the Babbitt Center is working on this and another pilot project in the Denver area, the hope is that the results will contribute to a global conversation around water-management experimentation.

And Allenby suggests that the "recipes" being devised by technologists, policymakers, and planners will ideally lead to a shift in more accurately evaluating the efficiency and impact of various land use projects. This, he hopes, will lead to the most important outcome of all: "Making better decisions." ❯

Opposite: A Center for Geospatial Solutions image combines spatial analysis with land parcel data to illustrate different types of property ownership in Baltimore.

Below: Mapping satellites range in size from less than a foot to a large SUV.

NEW SPACE SATELLITE HIERARCHY

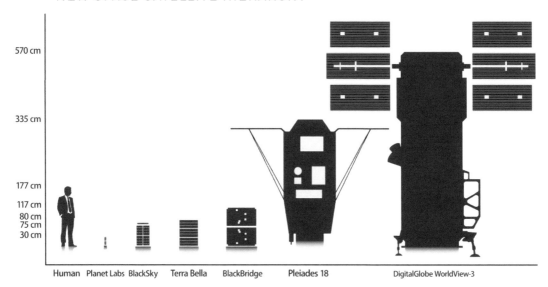

570 cm

335 cm

177 cm
117 cm
80 cm
75 cm
30 cm

Human Planet Labs BlackSky Terra Bella BlackBridge Pleiades 18 DigitalGlobe WorldView-3

PRECISION MAPPING WATER IN THE DESERT

THE LATEST

Technology moves fast, and mapping is no exception: the recent rise of artificial intelligence (AI) has led to significant changes in the industry, says Jeff Allenby. More companies are offering more AI-based mapping programs than ever before, Allenby says, but he notes that ensuring the precision of data is a serious concern as the market expands, warning that for some providers, "close enough is good enough." Allenby joined the Lincoln Institute of Land Policy in 2020 as a founding member of the Center for Geospatial Solutions (CGS) team, which helps organizations of all sizes use data to improve decision-making related to conservation, climate change, housing affordability, and other work to promote social equity. As Allenby, the director of geospatial innovation for the center, puts it, "CGS is a trusted advisor that plays matchmaker between organizations and the data they need." In addition to the mapping work in Pima County and Denver, the Babbitt Center's partnership with the Conservation Innovation Center included mapping projects for the Colorado Water Conservation Board and Grand Canyon Trust. The Babbitt Center continues to collaborate with partners both within and beyond the Colorado River Basin to advance the integration of land and water management.

LEARN MORE   **Babbitt Center for Land and Water Policy**
https://babbittcenter.org

Center for Geospatial Solutions
https://cgsearth.org

Conservation Innovation Center
https://www.chesapeakeconservancy.org/conservation-innovation-center

STREETLIGHTS ARE GETTING SMARTER— ARE WE?

The ubiquitous streetlight has begun to occupy a new role in the urban streetscape,

evolving from a simple source of light into a device that can do everything from collect data to charge vehicles. These advances are creating opportunities—and shedding light on the intersection of infrastructure and technology.

IN 1879, A DELEGATION of officials from Detroit took a steamship across Lake Erie to Cleveland, where they examined the nation's first electric streetlights. Three weeks earlier, inventor and engineer Charles Brush had flipped the switch on a dozen "arc lamps" in a public square in the latter city. "Most people seemed struck with admiration," reported Cleveland's *Plain Dealer* newspaper, "both by the novelty and brilliancy of the scene."

Detroit quickly embraced the new lighting technology, as did other major cities, including San Francisco and Boston. In other places, including Brush's own Cleveland, leaders debated whether to make the switch from gas lamps. (They were still arguing the point a few years later when Brush hired fellow Cleveland inventor John C. Lincoln to work at his company; the latter went on to found the Lincoln Electric Company and the Lincoln Foundation, which evolved into the Lincoln Institute of Land Policy.)

Previous: Newly upgraded LED streetlights in Detroit.

Below: LED bulbs in the Detroit Public Lighting Authority warehouse.

Eventually, of course, electric streetlights became ubiquitous. During the 20th century, streetlight technology evolved gradually, with the carbon rods

STREETLIGHTS ARE GETTING SMARTER–ARE WE?

in Brush's lamps giving way to Thomas Edison's incandescent bulbs, then to mercury and sodium bulbs. In the past decade or so, that evolution has accelerated dramatically, thanks to two developments. First is the emergence of light-emitting diodes (LEDs), which offer considerable energy savings. Second is the more recent explosion of interest in outfitting streetlights with "smart city" technologies that go well beyond lighting—think everything from surveillance cameras to Wi-Fi hotspots.

All of this underscores, and complicates, the often-overlooked role of streetlights in planning and land use. "A street lighting system is there for traffic safety, pedestrian safety, and to make people feel safe in cities where there may be high crime," says Beau Taylor, executive director of Detroit's Public Lighting Authority (PLA).

More than a century after it installed those innovative arc lamps, Detroit was essentially forced back to the leading edge of lighting. By 2014, some 40 percent or more of its 88,000 sodium streetlights had become nonfunctioning at any given time. The city's lighting infrastructure, spread over 139 square miles, had been designed for a thriving city of two million people in the 20th century. Maintaining it had become untenable.

A $185 million bond funded 65,000 new LED streetlights, making Detroit the first large US city to convert to LEDs. This upgrade was not just a matter

Smart streetlights can include components such as air quality sensors, charging stations for cars and electronics, security cameras, and motion detectors. Cities around the world have installed variations of the lights.

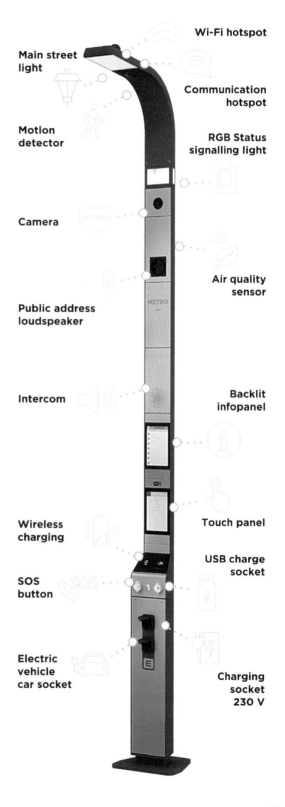

Main street light

Motion detector

Camera

Public address loudspeaker

Intercom

Wireless charging

SOS button

Electric vehicle car socket

Wi-Fi hotspot

Communication hotspot

RGB Status signalling light

Air quality sensor

Backlit infopanel

Touch panel

USB charge socket

Charging socket 230 V

Beau Taylor of Detroit's Public
Lighting Authority.

of swapping out bulbs. The lighting from LEDs is different—a sodium bulb produces light that gradually tapers, while LEDs produce a more direct shaft that's twice as bright—and Detroit's population has shrunk, so planners had to install new poles in a revised configuration.

Today the agency says the energy costs associated with the new lights are about half what they would have been with conventional lights. And an analysis by the Detroit Greenways Coalition, a policy and advocacy group, found that "pedestrian fatalities in dark, unlighted areas dropped drastically, from 24 in 2014 to just one in 2017," concluding that the new lights were the primary factor.

Those are significant outcomes. But there could be more to come: Detroit's new streetlights are equipped with fixtures that can be retrofitted to perform various "smart" functions. And this brings us to the technological revolution that has attached itself to the formerly humble streetlight.

"When we use the word 'smart,' it means connected," says Dominique Bonte, a vice president at consultancy ABI Research, which forecasts the smart streetlight market will grow 31 percent between 2018 and 2026. Lights that are connected by a network, whether Wi-Fi or fiber-optic cable, can be monitored or controlled remotely. These connections also open new possibilities, particularly as the more robust 5G cellular network technology rolls out over the next few years. "Streetlights, in the future, can become more like hubs or platforms," Bonte continues.

If streetlights are already on every block, why not figure out what else they can do?

Streetlights are ideal for this role, as Austin Ashe, general manager for intelligent cities at GE subsidiary Current, explained to engineering trade publication *IEEE Spectrum:* "They have power, ubiquity, and the perfect elevation—high enough to cover a reasonable radius, low enough to capture a lot of important data."

This notion has already captured the imagination of cities around the world: if streetlights are already on every block, why not figure out what else they can do?

A study by research firm IoT Analytics estimates the total number of connected streetlights in North America will reach as high as 14.4 million over the next five years, naming Miami as the city with the most extensive deployment of connected LED streetlights, with nearly 500,000. In Los Angeles, 165,000 networked streetlights are designed to serve as a kind of backbone for the deployment of other technologies, such as noise-detection sensors that monitor gunshots and other sounds. San Diego has tested streetlights outfitted with audio and visual surveillance technology, plus sensors that monitor temperature and humidity. In Kansas City, a new 2.2-mile downtown streetcar line is dotted with Wi-Fi kiosks, traffic sensors, and LED streetlights with security cameras attached, all linked by fiber-optic cable. And Cleveland is embarking on a $35 million effort to replace 61,000 fixtures with smart camera–enabled LED streetlights. Similar efforts are underway in Paris, Madrid, Jakarta, and other cities around the world.

But as these experiments play out, concerns are coming into view. The ACLU and others take issue with the idea of camera-enabled streetlights watching the public's every move, calling for government oversight to ensure that "smart cities" don't become "surveillance cities." As municipal enthusiasm for new technologies outpaces their regulation, some leaders are considering caution: "Technology is advancing at a rapid pace," a San Diego City Council member told the *Los Angeles Times*. "As elected officials, we have to not only keep up with the increasing developments, but also ensure that the civil rights and civil liberties of our residents are protected."

And then there are the economics of it all. Streetlights can eat up to 40 percent of municipal energy bills, according to the US Department of Energy, so basic efficiency upgrades tend to pay off over time. But as ABI's Bonte points out, the return on investment for more elaborate projects isn't always clear, and realizing the benefits can take decades.

Above: An electric car charges at a streetlight in Ireland. More than 10,000 such chargers are available in Europe, and the option is gaining speed in the United States.

Next: Protesters in Hong Kong tear down a smart streetlight in 2019 as part of an anti-surveillance demonstration.

"As elected officials, we have to not only keep up with the increasing developments, but also ensure that the civil rights and civil liberties of our residents are protected."

Looking ahead, Taylor of the Detroit PLA says his agency is tracking the experiments underway in other cities and participating in efforts to figure out which smart products or services might benefit the people of Detroit. If the city decides to, for example, add more public Wi-Fi in parks or other spaces, retrofitting the streetlights is an option. But that's in the future. "Smart city technology is more of a multiplier effect for a street lighting system," he says. "Our primary focus was getting the lights back on."

Even that comparatively cautious approach came with risks: In a frustrating development, the PLA found that lights supplied by one of its vendors were burning out far more quickly than they should. The city had to swap out those lights, at a cost of around $9 million, and sued the supplier.

No wonder Taylor seems happy to wait and watch as others experiment. The last thing a city wants, given the pace of technology, is to have to overhaul its smart system a decade from now. "It's not about getting it all done up front," he says. "It's about keeping options open." >

Opposite: Taking advantage of brighter LED lights in Detroit.

Below: A smart streetlight protester in San Diego carries a sign reading, "Cameras don't stop crime, well-fed communities do."

STREETLIGHTS ARE GETTING SMARTER—ARE WE?

THE LATEST

The future of the humble streetlight may have flickered a bit, but it still looks bright. In 2022, investment in "smart pole" and related tech infrastructure topped $10 billion, according to ABI Research, which forecasts that figure will rise to more than $130 billion by 2030. Existing or new streetlights, already necessary components of the urban landscape, are serving as distributed hubs for Wi-Fi projects, security systems, the deployment of 5G cellular networks, and even (experimentally) as electric vehicle chargers. Some projects have faced delays or pushback, especially when local concerns about the potential use of street-lights for surveillance arise, but perhaps because these projects tend to be more incremental, they have been less controversial than more radical smart city experiments. (See "Privacy, Equity, and the Future of the Smart City.") And improving technology is keeping the lights on longer, and more efficiently: Detroit, which gave its streetlights a citywide overhaul a few years ago, overcame early issues with one of its LED light suppliers, and its new system has proven far more reliable—a tangible example, the *Detroit Free Press* reported in 2023, of the city's promising post-bankruptcy progress.

LEARN MORE   **Sensing Lights: The Challenges of Transforming Street Lights into an Urban Intelligence Platform** (MIT Senseable City Lab)
https://senseable.mit.edu/papers/pdf/20220821_Alvarez-etal_SenseingLights_JUT.pdf

Streetlights Are Mysteriously Turning Purple—Here's Why (*Scientific American*)
https://www.scientificamerican.com/article/
streetlights-are-mysteriously-turning-purple-heres-why

What Is IoT: The Internet of Things, Explained (McKinsey)
https://www.mckinsey.com/featured-insights/mckinsey-explainers/
what-is-the-internet-of-things

PRIVACY, EQUITY, AND THE FUTURE OF THE SMART CITY

An ambitious development
proposed for the Toronto waterfront
planned to incorporate the latest
smart city technologies—

but it raised critical
questions about how
cutting-edge data
collection affects
our lives.

Above: Ann Cavoukian, former privacy commissioner of Ontario and advisor to a smart city project proposed in Toronto, developed the global "privacy by design" framework, which calls for privacy to be built into IT and infrastructure systems from the start.

Previous: A conceptual scale model of the proposed Quayside smart city development in Toronto.

AS A RULE, 12-acre development projects don't tend to receive national or international attention. But that hasn't been the case for Quayside, a parcel off Lake Ontario in Toronto. Two years ago, Waterfront Toronto—the government entity overseeing the redevelopment and reconfiguration of a larger swath of real estate along the Don River that includes Quayside—brought in Sidewalk Labs as a private partner. A subsidiary of Google's parent company, Alphabet, Sidewalk Labs pledged to invest $50 million in the endeavor. The company seemed an ideal choice to help make Quayside a kind of prototype "smart city" neighborhood and produced ambitious plans.

It also produced no small amount of controversy, and at times it appeared that the entire partnership might implode. All the friction had an unexpected result: Quayside could prove to be a much more valuable prototype for smart city planning than originally imagined.

That's not because of what has been built (which is, to date, nothing), but rather because the project's bumpy ride has clarified the core smart city issues that need to be resolved before any building can happen—not just in Toronto, but in any urban area. It's hard to find an example of a smart city project that's quite as comprehensive as Quayside aims to be, but there are many playing out on a more limited scale, from Kansas City's "smart city corridor" effort centered on a two-mile streetcar line to the LinkNYC program (also from Sidewalk Labs) replacing pay phones in New York City with Wi-Fi–enabled kiosks.

"There's no opportunity for people to consent or revoke consent. They have no choice."

The biggest issue needing resolution may be privacy. That may seem intuitive, and Sidewalk Labs itself professed to be aware of, and sensitive to, privacy concerns in its initial proposal. That proposal included plenty of the sort of tech-forward ideas you'd expect from a Google-connected entity, from heated bike lanes to autonomous delivery robots. Many of the proposed elements relied upon sophisticated sensors to collect data and guide efficiency in everything from trash collection to traffic to lighting.

While Sidewalk's proposal addressed privacy, the company was apparently caught off guard when it was criticized for leaving too much discretion to private-sector tech vendors. Among those unimpressed: former Ontario privacy commissioner Ann Cavoukian, a prominent privacy advocate Sidewalk had added to its advisory board who promptly resigned from that role.

Cavoukian, now the executive director of the privacy-focused Global Privacy and Security by Design Centre consultancy, explains that she recognizes the potential value of data collection for shaping a neighborhood or a city. But she believes, in essence, that in the context of the "smart" city, securing privacy is a planning-level decision better left to the public sector. "The technology, the sensors, will be on 24-7," she says. "There's no opportunity for people to consent or revoke consent. They have no choice."

She specifically advocates what she terms a "privacy by design" strategy, which scrubs data at the point of collection. For instance, cameras or sensors gathering traffic data might also pick up license plate numbers. If Cavoukian and other privacy advocates have their way, that level of personal data would simply not be collected. "You still have the value rendered from the [aggregate] data," she says. "But you don't have the privacy risks because you've de-identified the data." The essence of the privacy by design idea is that it privileges the public interest over private use of data; Cavoukian has pointed to the European Union's General Data Protection Regulation—which strictly protects individual privacy and has forced even the biggest tech players to adjust since its implementation in 2018—as a model.

Next: Public comment cards at the Sidewalk Labs information center in Toronto reveal some of the data privacy concerns shared by participants in public sessions.

Below: Smart city technologies on display at an event in Shenzhen, China.

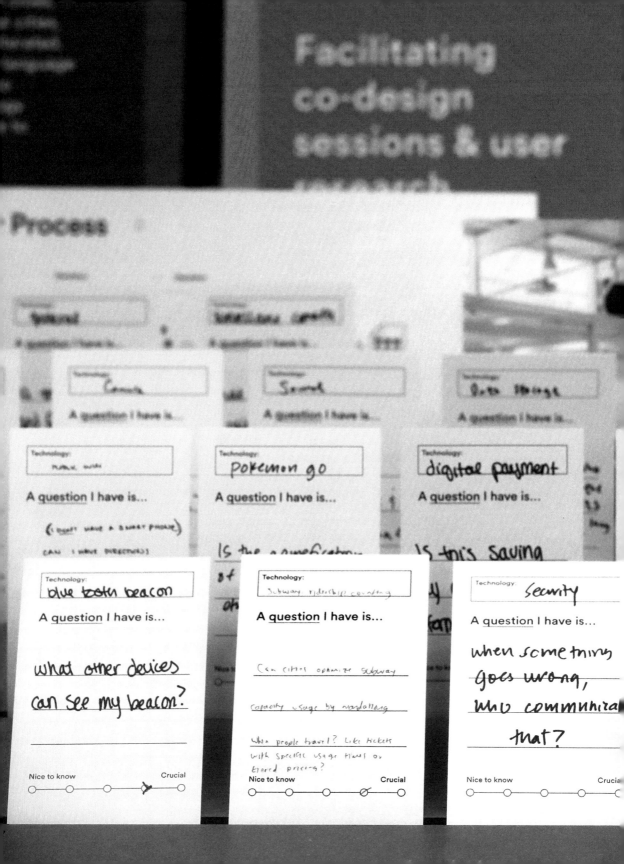

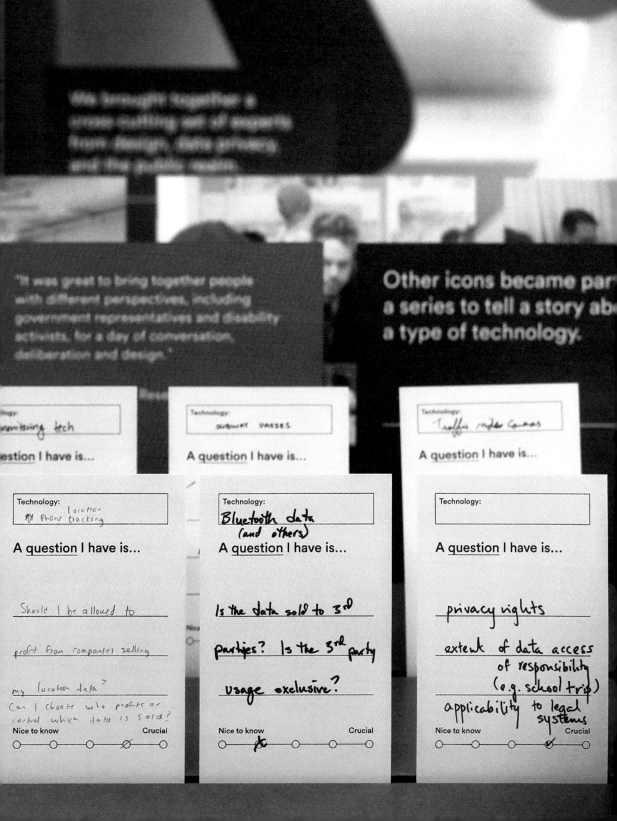

Sidewalk Labs proposed gathering wide swaths of data in a kind of "trust," with private vendors encouraged to anonymize data. To critics like Cavoukian, this delayed privacy decisions until too late in the process: post-planning, post-implementation, less a baseline than an afterthought. One poll found that 60 percent of Toronto residents who were aware of the plan didn't trust Sidewalk's data collection. The two sides eventually have agreed that sensor-gathered data would be treated as a public asset, not a private one. (Sidewalk Labs did not respond to an interview request.)

The Toronto proposal was controversial for other reasons. Notably, it sought oversight for much more than the original 12-acre parcel, dangling the possibility of locating a new Google Canadian headquarters along the city's waterfront as part of a scheme that would give Sidewalk latitude over 190 acres of potentially lucrative properties. This proposal was rejected, but spurred a useful debate about smart cities and equity.

Jennifer Clark, a professor and head of the City and Regional Planning Section at the Knowlton School of Architecture in the College of Engineering at the Ohio State University, has studied smart city efforts around the world and is the author of *Uneven Innovation: The Work of Smart Cities*, published by Columbia University Press. As she explains, technology businesses and government or planning entities come to these collaborations with distinct perspectives. Enterprises like Sidewalk Labs

In Kansas City, Missouri, a two-mile streetcar line is the center of a "smart corridor" equipped with Wi-Fi kiosks, smart streetlights, and traffic sensors.

PRIVACY, EQUITY, AND THE FUTURE OF THE SMART CITY

CENTRO DE OPERAÇÕES
PREFEITURA DO RIO

that are devoted to new city technologies, she says, "come from a particular orientation of thinking about who the 'user' is. They're very much thinking through a consumer model, with users and consumers as essentially the same thing. That's not how planners think about it in cities. Users are citizens."

Similarly, companies designing the technology meant to make a city "smart" are looking for a revenue model that will not just fund a given project but that can ultimately prove profitable—which guides the nature of their prototyping products and services that might be applied elsewhere. Clark points out that a seldom-discussed element of the smart city phenomenon is its "uneven implementation." Quayside and the wider waterfront redevelopment it is part of are expected to result in high-value properties, used and frequented by a demographic attractive to businesses.

"There's an assumption that if you do these urban development districts, you're experimenting on the model, you get the model right and then you do broad deployment, so that there's equity," Clark says. But frequently, in practice, "there is no path to that." Whatever innovations emerge tend to recur in demographically similar contexts.

What often underlies this dynamic is a kind of power mismatch. The private side of a development partnership is often richly funded, in a position to offer financial incentives, and thus to essentially dictate terms; the public side may have fewer resources, and less sophistication about assessing or

Officials monitor traffic, weather, and safety at Rio de Janeiro's Operations Center. The data hub, which integrates the work of dozens of agencies and has been called a "quintessential smart city project," was built after a devastating landslide caught residents unaware in 2010.

"We want a smart city of privacy."

fully deploying cutting-edge technology. But in this case, Clark notes, the Quayside story (which she addresses in her book) may be a bit different.

"Toronto has a history of community organizing and community development," she notes. "And the community organizations there have a sophisticated understanding of the data collection practices that were proposed." Thus the privacy pushback, and how it gets resolved, might prove to be the real lasting payoff, especially if it's resolved in a way others can emulate.

A replicable model, one that offers guidelines for both technology and the rules that technology must play by, is essentially the outcome that Cavoukian wants. She is now working with Waterfront Toronto and explicitly hopes that Quayside—with either Sidewalk Labs or new partners—can become a rejoinder to the surveillance-oriented versions of the smart city that are taking shape in tech-advanced urban areas from Shanghai to Dubai.

"We want to be the first to show how you could do this and put that out as a model," she says. "We want a smart city of privacy." ›

Opposite: Exploring plans at the Sidewalk Labs office in Toronto.

Below: At the Smart City World Expo Congress in 2021, a reminder to humanity to proceed with caution (left). Privacy by Design principles encourage a more sensitive approach to systems engineering (right).

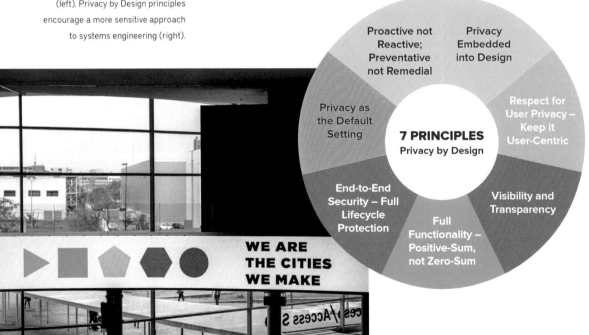

7 PRINCIPLES
Privacy by Design

Proactive not Reactive; Preventative not Remedial

Privacy Embedded into Design

Privacy as the Default Setting

Respect for User Privacy – Keep it User-Centric

End-to-End Security – Full Lifecycle Protection

Full Functionality – Positive-Sum, not Zero-Sum

Visibility and Transparency

WE ARE THE CITIES WE MAKE

THE LATEST

When this column was published, the collaboration between Toronto and Alphabet subsidiary Sidewalk Labs—arguably the most high-profile smart city development project to date—was at a crossroads. Just months later, its fate was sealed: Citing uncertainty stemming from the COVID-19 pandemic, Sidewalk's CEO announced that the project was no longer financially viable. But the effort had faced trouble long before the pandemic hit. In retrospect, the project did offer a beta test of a critical aspect of public-private smart city development: the struggle to balance the benefits of data collection against the peril of becoming a corporate surveillance state. Ann Cavoukian, executive director of the Global Privacy and Security by Design Centre, who became a prominent critic of the project, says that challenge remains. "When a city is working with a smart city [private-sector partner] that says it will ensure privacy is proactively embedded by design—be sure to get this in writing," she says, "along with the consequences of failing to do so." In Toronto, new plans for the waterfront are putting more of an emphasis on affordable housing and green spaces. Still, tantalizing visions of a techno-fied utopia built from scratch persist in other places, and have arguably become more grandiose: a project called California Forever, backed by Silicon Valley billionaires, aspires to devise a brand-new tech-infused city on farmland north of San Francisco. It remains to be seen whether the enterprise, which has already come in for criticism on aspects ranging from environmental impacts to social justice, learns some lessons from Sidewalk Toronto.

LEARN MORE

Global Privacy and Security by Design Centre
https://gpsbydesign.org

Toronto Wants to Kill the Smart City Forever (*MIT Technology Review*)
https://www.technologyreview.com/2022/06/29/1054005/toronto-kill-the-smart-city

Privacy Frameworks for Smart Cities (Mcity/University of Michigan)
https://mcity.umich.edu/wp-content/uploads/2023/03/Privacy-Frameworks-for-Smart-Cities_White-Paper_2023.pdf

INCREASE TREES 200% +

CONVERT STONE TO STABILIZED DECOMPOSED GRANITE

REDUCE GEOFOAM BY 60%

20% OF LAWN CONVERTED TO SHRUBS

NEW APPS ENCOURAGE CLIMATE POSITIVE DESIGN

1121

REMOVE SITE WALLS

Landscape architect Pamela Conrad couldn't find a tool to measure the climate impact of her work, so she created her own.

Hundreds of firms now rely on the Pathfinder app to help them create more sustainable, resilient places.

Previous: Landscape design choices can help reduce the carbon emissions of a campus, as illustrated by a Climate Positive Design case study.

Below: The Pathfinder landing page for De-Pave Park, a project that will—as its name suggests—remove the pavement from a former airfield in Alameda, California, and restore its original wetlands habitat.

A COUPLE OF YEARS AGO, landscape architect Pamela Conrad got curious about the climate impact of her work. How much carbon dioxide did her chosen materials release into the atmosphere? How much carbon was sequestered, or captured, by any given project's mix of trees, shrubs, grasses, and other plants? What factors could she adjust to improve the net outcome? Conrad, a principal at the San Francisco firm CMG Landscape Architecture, decided to investigate.

"I went online and I just assumed there was going to be some magical tool that I could download, and it would just tell me," she says. "I kind of expected to find it that afternoon." That didn't happen. She did find helpful tools and data intended to help gauge and improve the emissions impact of the built environment, but what she was looking for didn't seem to exist: a tool to help landscape architects understand, in a holistic way, the climate impacts of their work.

Beyond her personal curiosity, this struck Conrad as a surprising absence. "We haven't been measuring anything outside the building," she says. That meant crucial conversations with policymakers and clients weren't happening, because "we haven't had the data." Because landscape architecture can not only reduce emissions but also make tangible contributions to

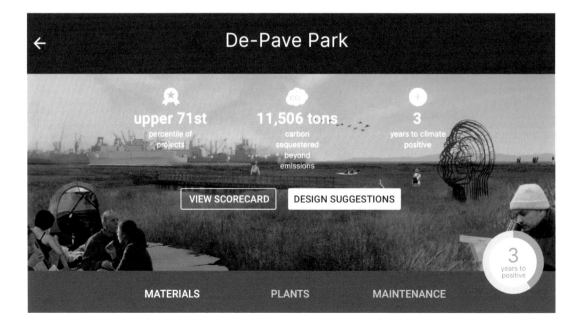

NEW APPS ENCOURAGE CLIMATE POSITIVE DESIGN

carbon sequestration, this field is perfectly positioned to offer "climate positive design," as Conrad calls it: design that sequesters more carbon dioxide than it emits.

Conrad set out to make the tool she couldn't find, with the support of a research grant from the Landscape Architecture Foundation. She worked with environmental consultants and tech developers to create a beta version of the free web-based app now known as Pathfinder. The app, which formally launched in September 2019, has been used by 300 firms and counting. It is intentionally simple and accessible. Users enter various details of a project, large or small, from a backyard garden to a city plaza. The interface asks for information about materials (e.g., sand, crushed stone), plant types (e.g., trees, lawn), and other details.

On the back end, the app draws on data from sources including the US Forest Service and the Athena Impact Estimator software created by the Athena Sustainable Materials Institute (ASMI) for building materials. It provides a kind of carbon profile for each project and offers suggestions to improve it, such as substituting a no-mow meadow for a lawn, or a wood deck for paving. The suggestions are intended to reduce the time it will take for each project to become carbon neutral, and then carbon positive. In the course of designing Pathfinder, Conrad tapped into a vein of similar efforts in other corners of the architecture and construction sectors that are contributing fresh insight to broader discussions of policy, planning, and land use. ASMI, a nonprofit collaborative, has been a pioneer on this front: since 2002 it has provided a variety of software tools that help designers measure the building, construction, and material impacts of their projects and materials.

Interest in this sort of resource is surging. Stephanie Carlisle, a principal at Philadelphia architecture firm KieranTimberlake, caused a stir with a lengthy call-to-arms essay in *Fast Company* on architects' contribution to climate change. New construction contributes massively to carbon emissions, she wrote: "Although it's become mainstream to discuss energy efficiency and advocate for minimizing those impacts, architects, engineers, and planners have yet to truly reckon with the magnitude and consequences of everyday design decisions."

Above: Landscape architect and Pathfinder creator Pamela Conrad.

Next: Mission Creek Stormwater Park in San Francisco, designed by CMG Landscape Architecture, where Conrad is a principal. The park, which combines three stormwater treatment gardens with public space, earned national recognition.

> "These efforts should be treated as the beginning of a conversation—not the end of it."

Carlisle says she has been heartened by the enthusiastic response to the essay. As it happens, KieranTimberlake introduced its own carbon measurement tool, Tally, a few years ago. Tally was designed to be folded into workflow processes, as a plug-in to a 3D modeling software commonly used in the industry called Revit. This means, Carlisle explains, that a designer can substitute and change material and other options. Tally allows architects to compare the climate impacts of various materials on a work in progress, then run a report on its potential carbon impact. "It tells designers where to spend their energy," she says. Some 200 firms now use Tally, and its sales rose about 150 percent last year.

Tally, a software plug-in developed by architecture firm KieranTimberlake and now owned by the nonprofit Building Transparency, allows architects to compare the climate impacts of various materials.

Tally, Pathfinder, and other similar tools fit into a broader trend of architects and landscape architects responding to climate change. "These [projects] are great pieces of the puzzle," says Billy Fleming, Wilks Family Director for the Ian L. McHarg Center at the University of Pennsylvania and a coeditor of *Design with Nature Now,* a collaboration between the university and the Lincoln Institute of Land Policy. "The core of [the

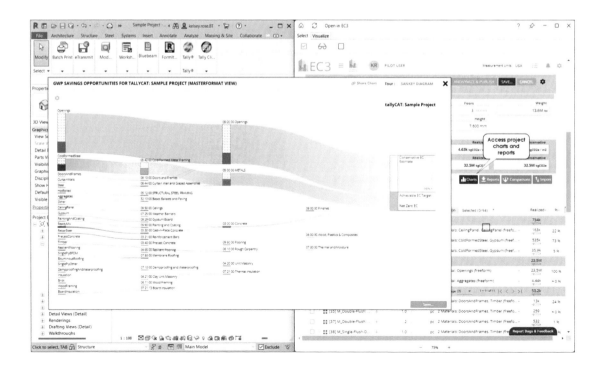

NEW APPS ENCOURAGE CLIMATE POSITIVE DESIGN

climate**positive**
design

challenge] is absolutely about social, technical, and political systems that have to be reorganized around an international mobilization and response to climate change. So these efforts should be treated as the beginning of a conversation—not the end of it."

Indeed, both Carlisle and Conrad emphasize that these tools are just a means to an end. Such tools are "directly empowering architects and engineers," Carlisle says, but they can also help establish common benchmarks that make it easier for communication around carbon standards to "make its way into policy and code." That's starting to happen—Carlisle cites Marin County's recent introduction of carbon standards for construction materials, and Conrad notes that San Francisco is embarking on a sustainable neighborhoods framework that factors in carbon sequestration standards—but they say there's still not enough awareness of the possible positive impacts of design outside the design professions, or perhaps even within them. "We need way more investment in R&D, and in tools," Carlisle says.

Conrad extends the point: as much as she intends Pathfinder to offer "really quick, accessible answers" with practical impacts on real projects, she also wants it to serve as an educational experience that builds awareness. "Landscape architects are the primary target," she says. "But I see [potential use for] a lot of other players in the space, like policymakers using it to set standards." While it's easy for an individual to use Pathfinder to plan a backyard renovation, large-scale landowners can use it to gauge the impact of setting aside portions of development for trees and other elements that

The basic tenets of Climate Positive Design hold that nature can help address much of the damage caused by humans.

SHIFTING THE PARADIGM

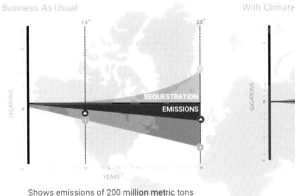

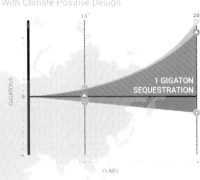

Business As Usual

With Climate Positive Design

Shows emissions of 200 million metric tons beyond sequestered by 2050

There is the opportunity to remove one gigaton of CO2 beyond emissions from the atmosphere by 2050

Above: Advocates of Climate Positive Design estimate that it could remove an additional gigaton of carbon from the atmosphere by 2050, beyond emissions reductions.

Opposite: Climate-resilient design in action at the Houston Arboretum.

build climate resilience. A simple slider interface shows the user that, for example, a combination of 400 large trees and 1,100 medium-sized ones can sequester 2.3 million kilograms of carbon. "Once we're able to measure what we're doing and collect that data and get that feedback," Conrad continues, "then we can start understanding what we're doing and evolve our practices."

Conrad has been spreading the word about Pathfinder through conferences and webinars, and has been taking suggestions that will guide updates in 2020. Late last year, she helped organize the Climate Positive Design Challenge, aimed at landscape architects, which established specific targets for projects large and small to achieve carbon-positive status: five years for parks, for instance, or 20 years for streetscapes or plazas. Pathfinder is meant to play a central role in helping designers meet that challenge.

"We think you can cut emissions on a given project in half, and increase sequestration by two or three times, just by having the right information in front of you."

"We could potentially take a gigaton of carbon dioxide out of the atmosphere over the next 30 years," Conrad says. "We think you can cut emissions on a given project in half, and increase sequestration by two or three times, just by having the right information in front of you." ❯

THE LATEST

Creating simple but accessible digital tools for landscape architects and others to gauge—and lessen—the potential carbon impact of their projects in the planning and design stage had enough potential by the late 2010s to inspire several experiments, pilots, and prototypes. Since then, "knowledge, interest, and demand around improving emissions and the tools to do so has increased exponentially," says Pamela Conrad, now the founder and executive director of Climate Positive Design. Pathfinder, the tool Conrad developed with environmental and tech experts, has been accessed by more than 10,000 projects in 131 countries, nearly double the figure from its first three years; student and education use has spiked as well. The international uptick has encouraged Conrad to keep the tool free and accessible. "I see it as one small way to support equity—for those that want to take climate action but can't afford it." Other tools are also seeing increased demand, and both industry and government partnerships are expanding. In 2024, Pathfinder plans an expansion to gauge biodiversity, water, and other project impacts. "We are on our way," Conrad says. "Now the question is, can we do it fast enough?"

LEARN MORE   ***Design with Nature Now*** (Lincoln Institute of Land Policy)
https://www.lincolninst.edu/publications/books/design-nature-now

Climate Action Commitment (International Federation of Landscape Architects)
https://www.iflaworld.com/ifla-climate-action-commitment-statement

Pathfinder (Climate Positive Design)
https://climatepositivedesign.com/pathfinder

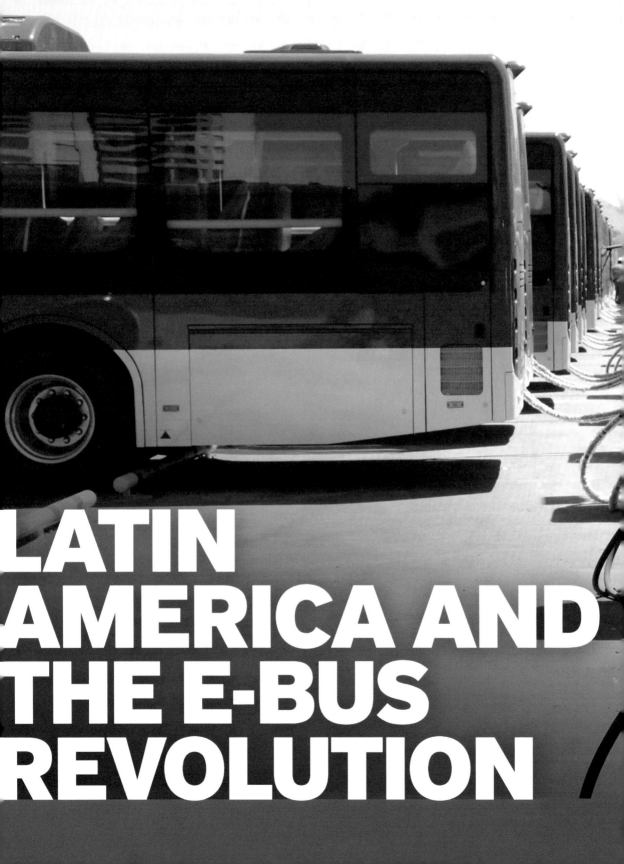

LATIN AMERICA AND THE E-BUS REVOLUTION

Santiago, Bogotá, and other Latin American cities are emerging as big players in the global electric bus market.

Motivated by the urgent need to combat air pollution and climate change, leaders are investing heavily in clean transit.

Above: Passengers disembark from an electric bus in Brazil. Innovative public-private partnerships have made Latin America a leader in e-bus adoption.

Previous: Electric buses at a charging station in Santiago, Chile.

AT SOME POINT IN THE LAST FEW YEARS, it was like a switch flipped: it became clear that the electric vehicle technology revolution is real and could have significant planning and land use impacts. For the last decade or so, the spotlight has often focused on how this cleaner energy alternative could power new ride-sharing and autonomous vehicle schemes, or micromobility innovations such as electric bikes or scooters. But some of the most illuminating electric vehicle experiments underway involve mass transit, including trains, trolley systems, and that most humble vehicle category, the city bus.

> Some of the most illuminating electric vehicle experiments involve mass transit, including trains, trolley systems, and that most humble vehicle category, the city bus.

While China is by far the global leader in building and using electric mass transit due to its state industrial policy and carbon reduction plan, Latin American cities are emerging as significant players in this growing market. By one estimate, more than 2,000 e-buses were operating in at least 10 countries across Latin America by the end of 2020. That number is

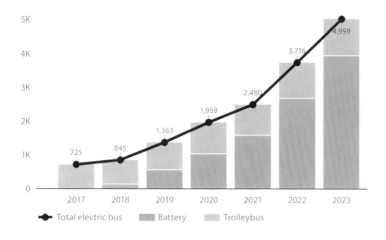

TOTAL OF E-BUSES IN LATIN AMERICA
(2023)

Chart data:
- 2017: 725
- 2018: 845
- 2019: 1,363
- 2020: 1,959
- 2021: 2,480
- 2022: 3,716
- 2023: 4,998

Legend: ● Total electric bus · Battery · Trolleybus

expected to rise: one analysis predicts that by 2025 the region will add more than 5,000 electric buses a year.

The push for electric buses is motivated by the urgent need to reduce the diesel emissions that cause air pollution and contribute to climate change. Widespread adoption is likely to have a significant impact, given that per capita public transit ridership is reportedly higher in Latin America than in any other region of the world.

A report from the International Finance Corporation (IFC), a global development organization that is part of the World Bank Group, and C40 Cities, a climate action coalition, pointed to two notable examples of cities investing heavily in electric buses. Santiago, Chile's capital city, has a fleet of more than 700 e-buses and growing, the largest outside of China. (By comparison, the entire United States had about 650 e-buses in 2020, although political momentum seems to be building for an investment in the sector.)

Santiago is aiming for a zero-emission fleet by 2035. In Colombia, Bogotá has undertaken an ambitious effort to put more than 1,000 e-buses into service, tied to Colombia's larger effort to cut carbon emissions 20 percent by 2030.

Both cities are using innovative public-private funding arrangements.

Above: Latin America's e-bus fleet has seen strong growth in recent years.

Below: Buses charge at a terminal in Santiago's Peñalolén district. A full charge takes two to three hours.

The region is known for embracing transit innovation, from electric trams in the 1950s to today's Bus Rapid Transit, propane taxis, and cable car lines that serve dense, hilly informal settlements.

As the IFC/C40 report points out, most municipal transit systems are owned either by a public agency or by a private operator with a municipal concession of some sort. But newer arrangements "unbundle" ownership and operation—essentially using the kind of leasing strategies familiar in, say, commercial airlines (where one set of companies makes planes, and a different set leases and operates them). "Asset owners own, and operators operate," as the report put it.

In Bogotá, for instance, the municipal transportation entity, Transmilenio, contracted with Celsia Move, an energy-focused subsidiary of multinational conglomerate Grupo Argus, to deliver the bus fleet. In turn, Celsia Move made a 15-year agreement with Grupo Express, a separate company, to

A worker inspects a circuit board at an e-bus factory in Rancagua, Chile.

operate and maintain that fleet. As John G. Graham, a principal industry specialist in the IFC's global transport group, explains, this unbundling makes each entity more attractive to different sets of potential investors. An owner entity can expect fixed payments, and its assets can be collateralized; an operator takes much less capital risk.

Electric buses and trains entail a much steeper up-front investment than their fossil fuel rivals—double the cost or more, by some estimates. But these recent public-private partnerships have reportedly attracted commitments from more than 15 investors and manufacturers, raising approximately $1 billion to deploy an additional 3,000 e-buses in various cities. International financing in support of e-bus and other green projects across Latin America has come from heavyweights like the InterAmerican Development Bank and the Partnering for Green Growth and the Global Goals 2030 initiative (P4G), whose initial funding came from the government of Denmark.

As Graham of the IFC points out, the underlying economics are also evolving. An electric bus can be cheaper to maintain over time, meaning that as battery technology improvements lower that up-front expense, the so-called "total cost of ownership" over a vehicle's lifetime should soon approach parity with internal combustion engine alternatives. Still, finding sustainable sources of support will be critical, given that financing major

Above: Most of Latin America's e-bus fleet has been imported, including these Yutong buses waiting to be shipped from a port in China.

Next: Passengers wait for an e-bus in Santiago.

In 2023, Santiago put a fleet of double-decker e-buses into service ahead of the Pan American Games. The buses are the first of their kind in Latin America.

transportation projects—including electrification upgrades—is invariably a challenge.

One option could be land-based financing. In Costa Rica, for example, the Lincoln Institute of Land Policy has worked with policymakers to explore land-based finance options to help offset the $1.5 billion cost of an expansion and electrification of a major train line serving the capital, San José. Throughout Latin America, notes Martim Smolka, a Lincoln Institute senior fellow and former director of its Program on Latin America and the Caribbean, land value capture strategies have been used to help fund major projects, such as redeveloping former factory and industrial zones. The value capture model ensures that a portion of the increase in land values that results from municipal actions is returned to the municipality to help offset the costs for other projects, such as improving local infrastructure.

"Transportation does help structure the value of land," Smolka says, but capturing that value can be trickier than with a more straightforward redevelopment project, given the scale of most transit projects.

Finding sustainable sources of support will be critical, given that financing major transportation projects— including electrification upgrades—is invariably a challenge. One option could be land-based financing.

One effective approach, he notes, is to increase density around particularly busy transit stops, encouraging fresh development but requiring developers who benefit from rezoning to, in effect, pay for the opportunity. He adds that an economic impact study commissioned by Costa Rica suggested the expansion of the electric train would have a positive effect on land values, and the project dovetailed with a pledge to reach carbon-neutral status by 2050.

Electric buses in London, Moscow, and Prague (top to bottom). Industry analysts predict that half the world's bus fleet will be electric by 2032, putting e-bus adoption a decade ahead of projected electric car adoption.

Latin America also has an increasingly strong trade relationship with China, which manufactures an estimated 98 percent of the world's total e-bus fleet.

Electric transit still represents just a sliver of all mass transit in Latin America, and the pandemic created new challenges. But the Latin American market may be particularly suited to capitalize on and expand this trend. Smolka observes that the region is known for embracing transit innovation, from electric trams in the 1950s to today's Bus Rapid Transit, propane taxis, and cable car lines that serve dense, hilly informal settlements. With relatively sophisticated transit authorities and a track record of financing major projects, "they are among the best transit systems in the developing market," says Graham.

Opposite: A quieter ride, faster acceleration, and more sensitive braking make driving an e-bus "a completely different feeling," said one driver in Sweden. "Like driving . . . a Jaguar!"

Below: A worker prepares wiring components at the Rancagua factory.

Among other things, that means lots of data on existing routes that can support the efficient deployment of new electric buses. It's much harder, Graham says, to "leapfrog" an electric system into a municipality with little transit track record than it is to phase the technology into an existing setup. Latin America also has an increasingly strong trade relationship with China, which manufactures an estimated 98 percent of the world's total e-bus fleet. All of this may be putting Latin America in a leadership lane for a transition that, in time, will happen globally. As Graham says: "Electrification is coming." ❯

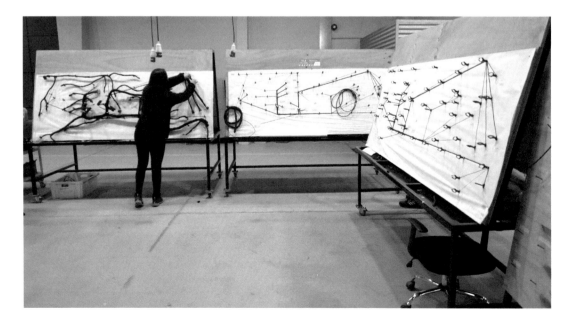

THE LATEST

Latin America's passion for electric buses has continued to grow. The global climate network C40 estimates that the number of e-buses in the region will increase from the 4,000 deployed on its streets by late 2023 to more than 25,000 by 2030. Santiago has maintained its role as an alternative transportation pioneer by further expanding its e-bus fleet, still the largest outside of China, and laying the groundwork for a pilot project that will test locally manufactured hydrogen buses. After years of relying heavily on imported buses to meet demand, the region is ramping up national production, especially in Brazil and Colombia. "Latin American cities are leading the way in the transition toward zero-emission transport that is equitable, accessible, and clean," says Ilan Cooperstein, C40's regional director for the region. While the electric train project in Costa Rica did not meet such a positive fate— President Rodrigo Chavez put the brakes on the ambitious undertaking two months after taking the reins in 2022—that country is now experimenting with e-buses too, thanks to a modest fleet that started with buses donated by the governments of Germany and China.

LEARN MORE   **Electric Bus Basics** (US Department of Transportation)
https://www.transportation.gov/rural/electric-vehicles/ev-toolkit/electric-bus-basics

Pipeline of Electric Bus Projects in Latin America: An Overview of 32 Cities (C40 Cities)
https://www.c40.org/wp-content/uploads/2023/10/Pipeline-of-Electric-Bus-Projects-in-Latin-America.pdf

Leading a Clean Urban Recovery with Electric Buses
(International Finance Corporation/C40 Cities)
https://www.ifc.org/en/insights-reports/2020/leading-a-clean-urban-recovery-with-electric-buses#

MANAGING THE CURB

When pandemic lockdowns scrambled the usage patterns of urban streets virtually overnight, cities responded with a wave of experiments and pilot programs. Many focused on reimagining curb management:

that is, making the most efficient use of space to respond to shifting demands for delivery, parking, and other uses.

AMONG ITS MANY CONSEQUENCES, the COVID-19 pandemic ushered in a period of experimental, rapid-fire adjustments to public space. Cities were suddenly tweaking zoning rules to allow more outdoor dining, blocking off streets to give pedestrians and bicyclists more space, and figuring out how to respond to dramatic upticks in food and retail pickup and delivery. It has been a pivotal stretch, in short, for managing the curb.

Even before the lockdowns began, the increasing popularity of transportation network companies—from ride-sharing services like Uber and Lyft to scooter firms like Bird and Lime—had made curb management a rising priority for many cities. "In today's urban fabric, few spaces are more contested than the curb," the American Planning Association declared back in the before-times of 2019.

But the welter of recent experiments, some involving deployment of new technologies, seems even more significant. Consider the case of Aspen, Colorado. Aspen is an unusual municipality, with a downtown business district that is geographically modest, at just 16 square blocks. Nevertheless, it's extremely busy: the retail and restaurant businesses there rack up a collective $1 billion a year. The inevitable upshot is that demand for curb space—for parking, for deliveries—can outpace supply. And that makes Aspen a useful curb-management lab.

The pandemic pushed a fast-forward button on new patterns of street usage and policy responses to those patterns.

In February 2020, Aspen joined a group of municipalities exploring pilot programs with a startup called Coord, one of several smart city tech companies with a curb-management bent. "I'm a data freak," explains Mitch Osur, Aspen's director of parking and downtown services. He figured that at the very least, Coord's platform—which integrates "smart zones" with a payment app used by delivery drivers (and a separate app for enforcement officers)—could give him fresh insight into how the downtown streets are really being used.

The city identified what it believed were its busiest loading zones. Starting in November 2020, using these zones required booking space through Coord's app, at a cost of $2 an hour. While regular street parking in downtown Aspen can cost $6 an hour, the city (like many others) had never previously charged for loading, but figured it was necessary to get delivery fleets' attention. In the end there wasn't much pushback; most drivers appreciated being able to capture a time slot. When one shipping fleet manager questioned the scheme, Osur explained that the shipper could use other loading zones, but the data Aspen was collecting would affect policy decisions about curbs across the downtown area. "If you're not part of the program, your data won't count," he added. Moreover, he was sharing data with participants and soliciting their input. The shipper signed on.

Because the Coord platform tracks actual usage of the smart loading zones, Osur did indeed get plenty of fresh data. Some was expected, some

Next: A mountain of packages reflects the surge in online shopping and home delivery during the pandemic. According to Adobe, online spending was 55 percent higher in 2020–2021 than in the two years prior.

Below: Anne Goodchild of the Urban Freight Lab (left), a public-private partnership housed at the University of Washington. The lab has partnered with cities including Seattle to research strategies for reducing dwell times in loading zones (right).

A pilot project in Las Vegas tested kiosks that monitored how much time cars spent in loading zones and alerted officials if the vehicles overstayed their welcome.

surprising. He figured average "dwell times" were about 30 minutes, and found they were averaging 39 minutes and 13 seconds. The dwell times were longer in the morning and shrank to about 15 minutes after 2 p.m. He was surprised to learn that the busiest days weren't Monday and Friday, as expected, but Tuesday and Thursday; Wednesday's loading zone use was half that of peak days. Based on these insights, Aspen is planning to change the rules for some zones, converting them to regular parking at 11 a.m. on some days rather than 6 p.m. (Osur has seen other changes that resulted from adopting Coord; drivers have stopped snagging space early and eating lunch in loading zones, a previously routine practice.)

Coord has run similar pilots in Omaha, Nashville, and other cities. But it is just one entity involved in curb-management experiments. Cox Communications, through its Cox2M Internet of Things division, is testing curbside kiosks that can essentially monitor dwell times in loading zones and present a countdown clock warning drivers not to overstay their time on the curb; the technology can alert city enforcement when drivers linger. Las Vegas is running a pilot program with the technology, which can also be used to manage commercial deliveries, a Cox official told *Government Technology*.

Columbus, Ohio, and Washington, DC, have run pilots with another app, curbFlow, designed to coordinate deliveries from multiple services along particularly busy curb stretches.

Before the pandemic, a curb change would have entailed lengthy public processes. The crisis showed that a more nimble alternative was possible.

Technology such as video kiosks and app-based location trackers adds both new options and new complexity to the business of managing curbs. Traditionally, defining curb use has involved signage and paint, which are hard to tweak quickly, notes Anne Goodchild, professor of civil and environmental engineering at the University of Washington, whose Urban Freight Lab has focused on public-private efforts to address evolving delivery logistics and planning.

Perhaps because of the pandemic, cities have been more willing to try new options. Before the pandemic, a curb change would have entailed lengthy public processes. The crisis showed that a more nimble alternative was possible. "We did some things differently," Goodchild says. "For example, we changed curb allocations literally overnight."

A curb regulation management solution developed by Esri for state and local officials as part of its ArcGIS web-based data mapping tool.

Curb management isn't merely an issue for downtowns or commercial districts . . . it tilts into residential neighborhoods as well.

The pandemic pushed a fast-forward button on both new patterns of street usage and policy responses to those patterns, says Heather Hannon, associate director of planning practice and scenario planning at the Lincoln Institute of Land Policy. During the pandemic, the organization's Big City Planning Directors Institute shifted from a twice-yearly gathering to a monthly one (held virtually, of course). The pandemic, she points out, "was a reason to try new things."

Hannon has observed a spike in interest in scenario planning for potential futures among US communities since the pandemic began. She also points out that curb management isn't merely an issue for downtowns or commercial districts, noting that it tilts into residential neighborhoods as well. The demand for home delivery has soared: food-delivery apps doubled their revenues in a six-month period during 2020 compared to the same period in 2019, and e-commerce in the United States grew 44 percent in 2020 compared to the previous year. These trends will only be complicated by the experiments with robots and drones that policymakers increasingly have to accommodate.

Aspen, meanwhile, has expanded its pilot program, adding new loading zones to the experiment as the number of participating drivers keeps growing. While it is just one experiment in a small city, it overlaps with a singular moment in the way citizens and businesses use technology to interact with planned spaces, opening a window onto how planners and policymakers might think about the future of the curb. "This is totally scalable," Osur says, referring not to any specific app or technology but to the general idea of cities using new tools to manage the curb more actively. "This is the future." ❯

Opposite: Turnover in loading zones increased 25 percent and double parking decreased 40 percent after officials in Pittsburgh, Pennsylvania, launched a test of camera-enforced time limits.

Below: Unloading a shipment in Aspen, Colorado. The city partnered with Coord on a pilot program that required drivers to reserve and pay for loading zone space.

THE LATEST

The fast-forward moment created by the pandemic has gradually faded, but urban street patterns haven't quite returned to a prepandemic status quo—and neither have efforts to use new data collection and other dynamic tools to tackle the long-vexing challenge of finding the right curb-use balance. Some experiments came and went quickly; Coord, the startup that ran ambitious tests in Aspen and other cities, no longer exists. But they all brought fresh attention to the curb as valuable and under-noticed urban space. In 2023, cities from Seattle to New York launched or announced new tests involving data-guided zone tweaks, micro-hubs for delivery vehicles, curb sensors, and dynamic pricing systems. And in early 2024, Aspen began seeking community feedback on a comprehensive effort to improve parking and transportation, replacing at-times conflicting solutions with a more holistic approach. Managing the curb, it seems, has evolved from a crisis into a crucial long-term project.

LEARN MORE   **Urban Freight Lab** (University of Washington)
https://urbanfreightlab.com

Create a Curb-Management Framework in Seven Steps (American Planning Association)
https://www.planning.org/planning/2022/winter/create-a-curb-management-framework-in-7-steps

Parking and Curbside Management Toolkit (Regional Plan Association)
https://rpa.org/work/reports/parking-and-curbside-management-toolkit

AS DELIVERY METHODS EVOLVE, WILL CITY STREETS KEEP UP?

The pandemic radically reconfigured the behavior and expectations shaping the way we use cities,

including the demand for all manner of delivery services. The market has chased that demand with new services, speedier logistics, and wholly different kinds of vehicles.

Above: The Nuro, a diminutive autonomous vehicle designed to haul up to 500 pounds of cargo.

Previous: Eric Joh, a deli owner in Ann Arbor, Michigan, loads sandwiches into an autonomous Refraction AI vehicle for delivery across town.

FOR YEARS, INNOVATIONS IN ALTERNATIVE MOBILITY—scooters, e-bikes, autonomous vehicles—have focused on how individuals get around. But the pandemic era has put fresh emphasis on a different mobility goal: moving *stuff* around.

The demand for rapid delivery has increased sharply in the past two years, and it doesn't seem to be abating. By some estimates, companies like DoorDash see the quick delivery of groceries alone adding up to a $1 trillion market. With major companies from UPS to Domino's trying out new ways to deliver their products, the pace and range of vehicle experiments has accelerated—and that is likely to impact the design, planning, and regulation of urban and suburban spaces.

While it's unclear which of these experiments will pan out, it's undeniable that new kinds of delivery vehicles are or soon will be on our streets. With new questions arising, urban design thinkers, retail and technology companies, and municipalities are working to address the convergence of increasing delivery demand and new vehicle forms. Leading the micromobility pack is the e-bike, a form that's been around for decades but has lately become strikingly popular: with sales up 145 percent since the pandemic started, e-bikes now reportedly outsell electric cars. John MacArthur, a program manager at Portland State University's Transportation Research and Education Center (TREC), has been researching their potential—including the "tantalizing hope" that micromobility tech gets more people out

of cars—for the better part of a decade. Last year, he taught a new class focused on cities dealing with all manner of new micromobility experiments, or "technologies being thrust in the public right of way."

Students in that class found that the pandemic was inspiring a range of responses from cities. On the one hand, work-from-home trends reduced and reconfigured car-centric commuter patterns. In Portland and else-where, MacArthur notes, that led to the creation of more bike and bus lanes. On the other hand, delivery demand spiked, leading to concern about a corresponding spike in single-occupancy delivery vehicles.

MacArthur's research connected him to Portland's B-Line Urban Delivery, a 12-year-old firm that operates a fleet of electric cargo trikes that can handle 500-pound loads. With input from TREC and B-Line, Portland is now con-sidering ways to create "microdelivery hubs." In this model, a truck brings a load of deliveries to a strategic location, with e-bikes or other microvehicles handling the last mile for each delivery, reducing traffic congestion. Such experiments are already underway in Europe, where delivery giant UPS has been experimenting with e-bikes, delivery hubs, and other "sustainable logistics solutions."

MacArthur acknowledges that complicated zoning and other issues are involved. But the bigger point is that Portland is among the cities proactively grappling with the future of mobility and how cities can

Above: Refraction AI cofounder and co-CTO Matthew Johnson-Roberson with one of the company's delivery vehicles in 2019. Johnson-Roberson became director of the Robotics Institute at Carnegie Mellon University in 2022.

Next: A fleet of Starship robots. Each is equipped with a suite of sensors and 12 cameras to navigate its delivery journey, which it makes at about four miles per hour.

respond to it and, more important, shape it. Shaping the response to new vehicle forms was a theme of a recent *Rebooting NYC* research project spearheaded by Rohit Aggarwala, a senior fellow at the Urban Tech Hub of the Jacobs Technion–Cornell Institute at Cornell Tech. Aggarwala—who previously led mobility work for Sidewalk Labs and recently joined New York City government as commissioner of the Department of Environmental Protection and the city's chief climate officer—sketches the broader context. "If a vehicle is designed to fit well in traditional traffic, then it is almost by definition not designed to be a good urban vehicle," he says. Cars, pickups, and SUVs are built for highways; their makers put far less emphasis on, say, turning radius or other factors that would make them more suited to the narrower confines of urban streets.

Thus the rise of new, smaller autonomous vehicles such as the Nuro, shaped like a diminutive van and about half the width of a conventional sedan; with no driver, it's designed to haul up to 500 pounds of cargo. The startup might be best known for a limited pilot program in Houston with Domino's, offering "the world's first fully automated pizza delivery service."

While such wee vehicles are pitched as virtuously reducing not just pollution but also traffic congestion, the reality is that they're often fundamentally unsuited to real-world traffic. So where can they go?

Another recent pilot program involving startup Refraction AI's REV-1 had the three-wheeled, washing machine–sized autonomous vehicle hauling pizzas via bike lanes in Austin, Texas—a development that some cyclists were not pleased about. "What if in two years we have

An illustration from the *Rebooting NYC* report shows how proposed New Mobility Lanes would accommodate both traditional cyclists and the emerging crop of delivery vehicles.

Before

Sidewalk | Bus Lane | Traffic | Traffic | Traffic | Parking | Bike | Sidewalk

Physical barriers to make it impossible for traditional vehicles to invade the New Mobility Lane

Simple posts that prevent vehicles wider than 6'6" from entering

After

15 MPH

Sidewalk | Bus Lane | Traffic | Traffic | Traffic | **Mobility Lane** | Sidewalk

Adopting a 10' standard would allow cyclists to pass each other comfortably and go around a cargo bike or AV shuttle that was stopping for a delivery or drop-off

several hundred of these on the road?" one bike advocate asked a local journalist. Yet another startup, Starship, has been testing its small mobile robot—a 55-pound object with the footprint of a wagon—in several cities, using sidewalks. This, too, has met with a mixed response. Such responses signal a major potential flashpoint, but also, perhaps, an opportunity. Aggarwala points out that in New York and other cities, bicy-

Dry cleaning delivery via electric cargo trike—coming soon to a neighborhood near you?

clists and e-bike users (who are often delivery workers) have long battled over bike lane use. In many cases, bike advocates have fought for years or decades to establish dedicated lanes and have little interest in seeing them clogged with newfangled motorized vehicles of any kind.

But the problem isn't the e-bikes or AVs or robots, each of which offers positive alternatives to traditional cars, Aggarwala says: "The problem is all these alternative vehicles being shoehorned into an incomplete network of generally unprotected lanes that are way too narrow." Thus the *Rebooting NYC* proposals include creating New Mobility Lanes. This would involve widening and expanding the city's existing bike lanes into a "network that can accommodate both bicycles and these new vehicles."

> "If a vehicle is designed to fit well in traditional traffic, then it is almost by definition not designed to be a good urban vehicle."

Other researchers have made similar proposals for "light individual transport lanes," with varying specifics but a common goal. "You're basically providing more space for different kinds of vehicles," says MacArthur of PSU. "That's the big question that planners will have to face in the next five years." It's a knotty challenge for municipalities caught between the ambitions of tech companies, the limits on local regulation resulting from superseding state or federal rules, and the reality that even designating

"You're basically providing more space for different kinds of vehicles. That's the big question that planners will have to face in the next five years."

bike lanes in the first place depends more on mustering political will and popular support than it does on the planning that underpins it.

On that last point, Aggarwala suggests a potential opportunity. As a political matter, bike lanes are often seen as benefiting just a portion of the population at the expense of everyone else. But pretty much everyone has been stuck behind a delivery vehicle. And, maybe more to the point, more of us than ever have come to depend on those delivery vehicles. So rejiggering the way road space is divided doesn't just benefit the few—it's for nearly everyone. In other words, Aggarwala asks: "What if you broaden the relevance of a bike lane by expanding its use?"

Clearly a wave of new-vehicle experimentation is poised to disrupt the delivery business, in a time of unprecedented demand. It's worth thinking about how planners and policymakers can not just respond to that wave, but harness it to help make city streets more functional and accessible for all. ❯

Opposite: Delivery by drone is increasingly common in Asia and is on the rise in other parts of the world.

Below: Bike-sharing, bike delivery, pedestrians, and vehicles share space on the streets of New York City.

AS DELIVERY METHODS EVOLVE, WILL CITY STREETS KEEP UP?

THE LATEST

Ongoing experiments with delivery logistics and vehicles are raising issues that planners and policymakers are still only beginning to grapple with. One concern that's drawing increasing focus is the climate impact of proliferating delivery vehicles. Portland, Oregon, for example, launched a pilot program in 2023 testing a Zero Emissions Delivery Zone and related digital infrastructure tools, notes John MacArthur, program manager at Portland State University's Transportation Research and Education Center. Meanwhile, vehicle technology potentially impacting the delivery economy continues to evolve, from the growing role of self-driving cars to the global expansion of delivery by drone—a relatively common practice in Asian cities that is gaining momentum in North America and other regions.

LEARN MORE

Transportation Research and Education Center (Portland State University)
https://trec.pdx.edu

Jacobs Technion–Cornell Institute (Cornell Tech)
https://tech.cornell.edu/jacobs-technion-cornell-institute

Rebooting NYC (Cornell Tech)
https://urban.tech.cornell.edu/rebooting-nyc

DESIGNING DASHBOARDS FOR LOCAL CLIMATE GOALS

Climate change is a global challenge that will shape and be shaped by local planning decisions.

Grappling with that complex reality has inspired the development of tools designed to help communities measure and reduce their emissions.

Above: A new online tool allows officials to track emissions in Minneapolis, where light rail and other transit options are helping to reduce greenhouse gas emissions.

Previous: A climate protester in Natick, Massachusetts. The town has used an online inventory tool developed by Boston's Metropolitan Area Planning Council to track its greenhouse gas emissions.

IN THE INCREASINGLY URGENT EFFORT to curb greenhouse gas emissions and slow the damaging effects of climate change, local policymakers and planners are playing a critical role. The good news is they have access to more data than ever. But wrangling, sorting through, and making sense of all this data can be a major challenge. A new crop of technological tools is helping to capture data related to municipal greenhouse gas emissions, organize it comprehensibly, and make it easy for municipal leaders to access.

In Minneapolis–St. Paul, the Twin Cities Metropolitan Council is working on an ambitious new effort to support local climate decisions. According to the Environmental Protection Agency, Minnesota's emissions per capita as of 2016 were slightly above the national average of 16 metric tons of carbon dioxide per person. But breaking down the details behind that number can be complicated. Simplifying it is a major goal of the council, which is a regional policymaking body, planning agency, and provider of essential services including transit and affordable housing for a seven-county region that includes 181 local governments.

In the works for several years, the Metropolitan Council's Greenhouse Gas Strategy Planning Tool grew out of the council's work to promote regional livability, sustainability, and economic vitality, and is ultimately intended for use by any municipality in the United States.

Intriguingly, the process began by assembling a team of partners including several leading academics (from Princeton University, University of Texas at Austin, and the University of Minnesota) studying various aspects of

DESIGNING DASHBOARDS FOR LOCAL CLIMATE GOALS

The council's simple web tool is designed to show in clear, graphic form the difference in emissions levels that would result from adopting specific tactics versus continuing the status quo.

climate change, as well as private sector nonprofit partners—"giving us access to all the science and innovation that academia can bring, combined with the practical wisdom of government," says Mauricio León, senior researcher for the Metropolitan Council.

León's duties include greenhouse gas emissions accounting for the Twin Cities region, which makes him familiar with the complexities of both measuring emissions in the present and figuring out how to project that data into the future under different scenarios. The council's recognition that this can be a time- and resource-consuming challenge for local governments led to the idea of building a web application that draws on existing databases and is adjustable according to specific policy strategies.

León and one of the council's partners, Professor Anu Ramaswami— a civil and environmental engineering professor at Princeton who has been the principal investigator in the planning tool project—emphasized that such public/academic partnerships don't happen often. "This is rare," says Ramaswami, who has worked with individual cities for years, but seldom on a project meant to serve such a broad range of municipalities and local governments.

In terms of the process, she says, scientists and policymakers jointly framed the relevant questions, then built the model together. The collaborators identified datasets related to the primary sources of emissions. In the

Next: Interstate 35 and downtown Minneapolis.

Below: A sample chart from the beta version of the Metropolitan Council's greenhouse gas scenario planning tool shows the relative impact of emissions reduction strategies.

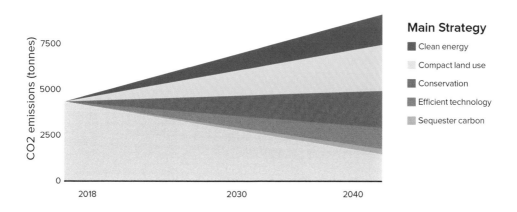

Main Strategy

- Clean energy
- Compact land use
- Conservation
- Efficient technology
- Sequester carbon

Solar panels installed at Natick High School in 2019, part of an effort by the town to reduce emissions and save on utility costs.

Twin Cities area, for example, 67 percent of direct emissions comes from "stationary energy" such as the electricity and natural gas used to power homes and buildings, while 32 percent comes from on-road transportation. The team also identified the most promising reduction and offset strategies and policies, including regulations, economic incentives, public investments, and land uses such as parks and greenways. With three focus areas or modules—building energy, transportation, and green infrastructure—the application is designed to show policymakers the potential outcomes of various mitigation strategies. The overarching framework is pegged to the goal of local governments achieving zero emissions by 2040, an aspirational target adopted by the Metropolitan Council.

In a preliminary conceptual demonstration of the tool at the Lincoln Institute's Consortium for Scenario Planning (CSP) conference, León showed how different types of communities, from cities to rural areas, will have different impacts and strategy options. A city has a lot of transit options, for example, that a rural community doesn't have. Policymakers using the tool can also factor in other key considerations, such as the equity implications of greenhouse gas reduction strategies that may impact some segments of a community more than others. "You can use this tool to create a portfolio of strategies that's based on your values," León explained.

With similar goals but a different approach, Boston's Metropolitan Area Planning Council (MAPC) unveiled a localized greenhouse gas inventory tool several years ago. MAPC's tool focuses less on future scenarios and more on providing community-specific, accurate baseline data and estimates of the impacts of various activities and sectors. Guided in part by a greenhouse gas inventory framework developed by the World Resources Institute, C40 Cities, and ICLEI-Local Governments for Sustainability, it attempts to measure a municipality's direct and indirect emissions.

Jillian Wilson-Martin, director of sustainability for Natick, Massachusetts, says the MAPC effort made available data and estimated impacts of car emissions, home heating, lawn care, and other factors that would be difficult for an individual town to collect. This helped Natick gauge its biggest sources of emissions, the first step in devising strategies to reduce them. Paired with offsets, the town aims to reduce its net emissions from nine metric tons per capita to net zero by 2050. "It's making it easier for smaller communities with no sustainability budget to get this really important data so they can be more effective," Wilson-Martin says.

Caped crusader Jillian Wilson-Martin, director of sustainability for the town of Natick, Massachusetts.

While MAPC provides guidance and training resources to the 101 cities and towns it serves in eastern Massachusetts, it's up to leaders in each municipality to customize how they measure their local emissions inventory, and how they might use that for planning. This may limit specific forecasting uses, but has another payoff, says Tim Reardon, director of data services for MAPC. "Ultimately, the value of having a nuanced and locally tailored tool is to gain credibility and buy-in with stakeholders at the local level," Reardon explained at the CSP conference. While big-picture data that doesn't apply to a particular community can be a turn-off, he said, local data brings the global climate crisis down to the ground and reduces a barrier to talking about what must happen locally to ensure a resilient future.

Often in discussions around greenhouse gas scenario planning, León agrees, "there's this element of 'this is just too complex for us to even think about.'" The council's simple web tool is meant to help counter that argument. It's designed

to show in clear, graphic form the difference in emissions levels that would result from adopting various specific tactics versus simply continuing the status quo.

One benefit of such an accessible tool, Ramaswami adds, is that it encourages wider involvement and thus "opens up more creative opportunities." In fact, she says, the project has had a similar effect on its academic partners: "It requires a different kind of research mentality, and a different kind of research group" to work directly with municipalities and respond to real policy options. When the tool is released, it will be accompanied by the publication of related academic research from Ramaswami and the group's other scholarly partners.

León acknowledges that the application will have its limits and that, ultimately, more sweeping federal and global policies will have greater total impact than any single local initiative. But anything that boosts engagement is important, he says. And the web application is designed to encourage municipalities of all sizes to interact with the calculations and numbers the project team has compiled; they won't have to upload their own data. "It's really easy," León says, "and there's no excuse for them not to use it." ❯

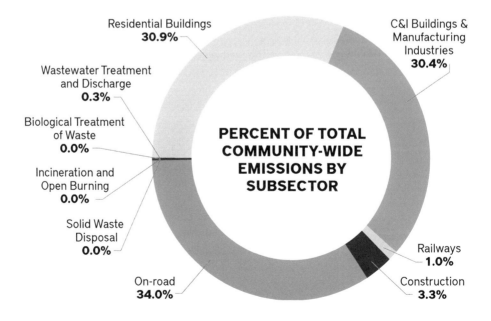

Residential Buildings
30.9%

C&I Buildings & Manufacturing Industries
30.4%

Wastewater Treatment and Discharge
0.3%

Biological Treatment of Waste
0.0%

Incineration and Open Burning
0.0%

Solid Waste Disposal
0.0%

On-road
34.0%

Railways
1.0%

Construction
3.3%

PERCENT OF TOTAL COMMUNITY-WIDE EMISSIONS BY SUBSECTOR

THE LATEST

The Twin Cities Metropolitan Council's Greenhouse Gas Strategy Tool was released in late 2023. "The tool is a significant step forward, using customized local data from various sources to model future emissions and compare mitigation strategies," says former council researcher Mauricio León, now the carbon reduction manager for Hennepin County, Minnesota. The Environmental Protection Agency has also made a local-focused tool available. León concedes that despite "keen interest" from cities in such tools, challenges remain in synthesizing data and policy. Such tools and experiments have to be scrupulously updated and maintained to have practical impact, notes Jillian Wilson-Martin, director of sustainability for Natick, Massachusetts. But she's seen more efforts to make better data more widely available, noting that her state's transportation department has released a useful vehicle census that wasn't previously available to help shape greenhouse gas impact studies. "It is great to see state governments taking action," she says, "to make their data more readily accessible at the local level."

LEARN MORE **Greenhouse Gas Strategy Planning Tool** (Metropolitan Council, Minneapolis)
https://metrotransitmn.shinyapps.io/ghg-strategy-tool

Community Greenhouse Gas Inventories (MAPC, Boston)
https://www.mapc.org/planning101/community-ghg-assessment

Local Greenhouse Gas Inventory Tool (EPA)
https://www.epa.gov/statelocalenergy/local-greenhouse-gas-inventory-tool

NEW ANGLES ON NOISE POLLUTION

In the urban context, noise tends to get attention when it is framed as a quality-of-life annoyance. But its impact can be much more profound, as new tools are demonstrating.

Above: *Quel* noise! A child reacts to traffic in Paris.

Previous: Flying low in Tokyo.

CITY DWELLERS AROUND THE WORLD noted one surprisingly welcome side effect of the lockdown phase of the pandemic era: less noise. Urban soundscapes have largely returned to form, but that peaceful interlude served as a loud and clear reminder to planners and policymakers that the audible does shape city life—and can, in turn, be shaped by policies that include thoughtful land use and design. Inger Andersen, executive director of the United Nations Environment Programme, highlighted the issue in the *Financial Times*, writing that "city planners should take both the health and environmental risks of noise pollution into account."

Of course, the underlying insight here is not new. Citizens have probably complained about various forms of city noise, from construction to concerts to rude neighbors, for as long as cities have existed. While a relatively quiet urban neighborhood might register an ambient level of about 50 decibels, higher levels can begin to interfere with conversation; a busy roadway can measure about 70 decibels (about equal to a vacuum cleaner), and a train crossing that road can push the decibel reading to 90 or higher.

Studies documenting the health effects of noise pollution, which range from sleep disturbances to cognitive issues to heart disease, date back at least to the 1970s. The World Health Organization, along with regulators in the United States, Europe, and elsewhere, has highlighted the issue for decades, often spurred by a panoply of noise activists.

Most cities already have some sort of noise ordinances in place, but such rules are rarely enforced in a systematic or consistent way. The advanced new sensors could help remedy that.

"The good news is there is much more interest today," says Arline Bronzaft, a City University of New York professor emeritus who conducted some of the earliest studies documenting the impact of city noise on health and well-being. Trained as an environmental psychologist, Bronzaft continues to advocate for quieter built environments as a board member of the environmental nonprofit GrowNYC. Today, she says, there's much more research, and an openness to policy experimentation. "Now that you've got the data," she says, the question is becoming: "what are you doing about it?"

The answer is a work in progress, but we may be at a pivotal moment for thinking about what might be termed "built soundscapes." The tools available to assess the challenge have radically improved. And that may help planners and policymakers devise and enable better design and policy strategies to cope with the problem.

Maybe the most prominent example involves the evolution of tools to measure sound, which have become more sophisticated and are being deployed in new ways. Recently, for example, authorities in Paris and other French cities have begun to experiment with "sound radar" devices meant to function like speed cameras: triggered by noise that exceeds code decibel limits, the sensors photograph the offending vehicle's license plate and fine the owner.

The French sensors were developed by Bruitparif, a state-backed agency devoted to studying city acoustics in Paris and elsewhere. Similar technology is being tested in New York, Edmonton, and other cities. Most cities already have some sort of noise ordinances in place, but such rules are rarely enforced in a systematic or consistent way. The advanced new sensors could help remedy that.

Next: A sensor equipped with microphones and a camera monitors traffic noise in Paris, reporting the license plates of violators.

Below: Environmental psychologist Arline Bronzaft measures sound levels along New York City's FDR Drive in 1995.

Erica Walker, professor of epidemiology at Brown University and founder of the Community Noise Lab, mapped noise levels around Greater Boston and developed the NoiseScore app.

Still, there's an argument for going deeper in thinking about sound—using technology as a planning tool, not just a punitive one. Erica Walker, professor of epidemiology at the Brown University School of Public Health and founder of Brown's Community Noise Lab, spent years creating the "2016 Greater Boston Noise Report," mapping noise data she collected at some 400 locations around the city. The experience gave her a different perspective on soundscapes.

"I started as pro-quiet," Walker says. In fact, she explains with a laugh, she was partly interested in finding out whether city noise codes might help her get some loud neighbors to pipe down. Creating her noise report brought Walker into contact with a cross section of situations, teaching her that "neighborhoods and sound are complex." Because ordinances focus almost exclusively on sound as a nuisance, they're often incomplete or counterproductive, she explains. Since some level of sound is inevitable in a city, Walker says, considerations of how the acoustic environment affects residents and their interactions with each other should be built into planning and development: "Now I'm anti-quiet—but for peace."

Her Community Noise Lab project is focused on reworking the soundscape dialogue between citizens and policymakers; among other initiatives, that has included creating a free app called NoiseScore to make sound measurement an accessible, collaborative activity. City officials in Asheville, North Carolina, used the tool as part of their effort to incorporate more community feedback into revisions to the city's noise code, which was updated in the summer of 2021. While that still boils down to crafting ordinances, it's an example of technology broadening the discussion, rather than simply serving as an enforcement tool. "They didn't start with: 'We're going to put these sensors up across the city and punish people if they are doing this or that,'" Walker says. "They wanted to understand all of the partners' perspectives."

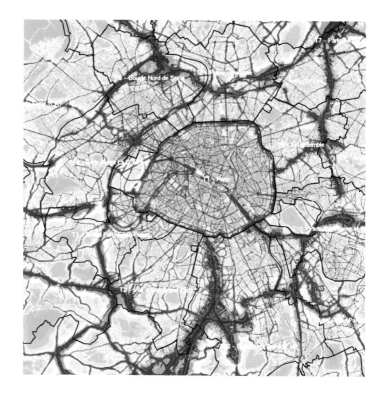

Tor Oiamo, a professor in the Department of Geography and Environmental Studies at Toronto Metropolitan University who conducted a recent public health noise study in that city, notes that more sophisticated sensors, mapping, and modeling software are creating opportunities to plan with sound in mind. In the years ahead, he says, the tools at hand could include a kind of global noise database similar to those tracking air pollution. But there's an obvious challenge: "The difficulty in mitigation with a city that's already built is that the structure is in many ways locked in," he says.

A map of noise levels in Paris over the course of a full day.

In some cases, cities have found ways to modify or add to existing infrastructure. Bronzaft's groundbreaking research in the 1970s—she documented the negative impact of a New York subway traveling on an elevated line near a school—resulted in the installation of sound-muffling acoustic tiles in classrooms, and the use of rubber pads on tracks throughout the subway system to lessen train noise. Other train systems now use rubber tires, and the next wave of quiet mass-transit innovation includes maglev (magnetic levitation) trains and electric buses.

Oiamo also points to successful efforts in Amsterdam and Copenhagen to revise traffic patterns, with the specific goal of reducing noise in residential zones. And he credits Toronto with a thoughtful approach to its current Port Lands development project: because it's reminiscent of a master-planned neighborhood, it's possible to factor the soundscape into the design process. In addition, many of the most measurably useful ways to mitigate urban noise overlap with thoughtful land use: more green space and trees, careful consideration of building density (strategic density can actually create pockets of quiet), and so on.

Land works have been used to mitigate urban noise for years, from the berms around the edges of New York's Central Park to trees and sound barriers along highways. A more recent tech-forward iteration comes from

Strategic density can actually create pockets of quiet.

German firm Naturawall, which has designed "plant walls"—galvanized steel frames with a relatively slim profile, filled with soil and sprouting a thick layer of foliage and flowers. The walls, currently in use in some German cities, are said to block sound levels roughly equivalent to typical city traffic. Other companies, including Michigan-based LiveWall, are undertaking similar projects around the world.

None of these strategies offers a silver bullet. But Oiamo, like Bronzaft and Walker, emphasizes that at this point, there is plenty of expertise to draw upon to improve our built soundscapes. Newer technologies are helping define the issues with greater nuance and offering fresh solutions. While sensors helping issue tickets for noise violations may not represent the kind of holistic approach Walker or Bronzaft have in mind, they're a start. As the subject gets more attention and technological options proliferate, sound-scape experts are sensing the potential for real, if incremental, progress. "There's a million things to do," says Oiamo. That's the challenge—and the opportunity. ❯

Opposite: Companies including Naturawall have developed plant walls that muffle traffic sounds and other noises.

Below: Protesters rally for a quieter Barcelona in 2022. The city installed sound monitors after a study found that 57 percent of residents are regularly exposed to noise levels exceeding World Health Organization guidelines.

THE LATEST

While the technology to both measure and mitigate noise has advanced considerably, the thinking about noise on a planning and policy level still tends to be narrow, treating it as a specialized issue rather than one that's integral to health and equity. Erica Walker, professor of epidemiology at the Brown University School of Public Health, has lately responded to this challenge by expanding the purview of the Community Noise Lab she founded at Brown. A second location for the lab was beginning its work in Jackson, Mississippi, when the failure of a water treatment plant plunged the city into crisis in 2022, forcing 150,000 residents to rely on bottled water. "So we switched gears," Walker says. The lab now also operates a tap water testing facility, and launched a long-term children's health study that tracks hearing, but also cortisol levels and other biometrics. More recently, it has expanded to study smaller communities in Mississippi affected by industry and illegal dumping, measuring air, water, and noise pollution. "We're looking at the total environment" says Walker, who grew up in the state—and that's become an intentional strategy to pull noise in from the margins. "It's everywhere. Noise is always in the mix. So we're connecting it to other things that can help to raise the urgency of recognizing it as an environmental stressor."

LEARN MORE

Community Noise Lab
https://communitynoiselab.org

The Growing Movement Against Noise Pollution (NPR)
https://www.npr.org/2023/08/19/1194882122/
the-growing-movement-against-noise-pollution

The World's Cities Must Take on the Cacophony of Noise Pollution (*Financial Times*)
https://www.ft.com/content/ffacda24-da6e-4a95-9ce5-a3343e23bc06

IS WOOD THE WAY OF THE FUTURE?

Mass timber—wood layered and treated to create a hardy construction material through special manufacturing techniques— is proving its mettle as a more carbon-friendly alternative to concrete and steel.

How does this new building option stack up?

WHEN YOU THINK ABOUT INNOVATIONS in development and construction, wood probably doesn't leap to mind. It is, to put it mildly, an old-school material. But "mass-timber" construction—which involves wood panels, beams, and columns fabricated with modern manufacturing techniques and advanced digital design tools—is sprouting notable growth lately. Advocates point to its potential climate impact, among other attributes: using sustainably harvested mass timber can halve the carbon footprint of a comparable structure made of steel and concrete.

According to wood trade group WoodWorks, more than 1,500 multifamily, commercial, or institutional mass-timber projects had either been built or were in design across all 50 states as of September 2022—an increase of well over 50 percent since 2020. The *Wall Street Journal*, citing US Forest Service data, reports that since 2014 at least 18 mass-timber manufacturing plants have opened in Canada and the United States.

The building blocks of mass-timber construction are wood slabs, columns, and beams. These are much more substantial than, say, the familiar two-by-four, thanks to special processes used to chunk together smaller pieces of wood into precisely fabricated blocks. The end result includes glue-laminated (or "glulam") columns and beams, and cross-laminated (or CLT) slab-like panels that can run a dozen feet wide and 60 feet long. The larger panels are mostly used for floors and ceilings, but also for walls. The upshot, as the online publication *Vox* put it, is "wood, but like Legos." Major

IS WOOD THE WAY OF THE FUTURE?

Building a 20-story structure of concrete would emit more than 1,200 tons of carbon, while building it with wood would sequester over 3,000 tons.

mass-timber projects tend to showcase the material, resulting in buildings whose structural elements offer a warmer, more organic aesthetic than do steel and concrete.

Both the process and interest in wood's potential have been building momentum for a while. Pioneered in Austria and used elsewhere in Europe since the 1990s, the practice has gradually found its way to other parts of the world. In an often-cited 2013 TED Talk, Vancouver architect Michael Green made a case for this new-old material: "I feel there's a role for wood to play in cities," he argued, emphasizing mass timber's carbon sequestration properties—a cubic meter of wood can store a ton of carbon dioxide; building a 20-story structure of concrete would emit more than 1,200 tons of carbon, while building it with wood would sequester over 3,000 tons. Plus, mass-timber structures can withstand earthquakes and fire.

When Green gave his talk in 2013, the tallest mass-timber structures were nine or 10 stories high. But Green argued this new fabrication process could be successfully used in structures two or three times that height. "This is the first new way to build a skyscraper in probably 100 years or more," he declared, adding that the engineering wouldn't be as hard as changing the perception of wood's potential. Lately that perception has been getting a

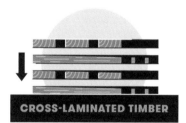

CROSS-LAMINATED TIMBER

NAIL-LAMINATED TIMBER

The wood layers that make up mass timber are typically held together with glue, nails, screws, or dowels. The number of mass-timber projects in the United States increased more than 50 percent between 2020 and 2022.

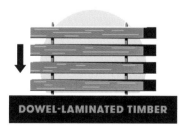

DOWEL-LAMINATED TIMBER

GLUE-LAMINATED TIMBER

fresh boost thanks to a spate of eye-catching projects—including a 25-story residential and retail complex in Milwaukee and a 20-story hotel in northeastern Sweden—and proposals for even taller mass-timber buildings.

Because mass timber is prefabricated in a factory and shipped to the site, unlike concrete structures made in place, the design details must be worked out precisely in advance, requiring intense digital planning and modeling. This can ultimately make construction processes more efficient, with fewer workers and less waste. Most mass-timber projects still incorporate other materials, notes Judith Sheine, an architecture professor at the University of Oregon (UO) and director of design for the TallWood Design Institute, a collaboration between UO's College of Design and Oregon State University's Colleges of Forestry and Engineering that focuses on advancing mass-timber innovation. "But mass timber can replace steel and concrete in many, many applications, and it's becoming increasingly popular," she says. "That's due to new availability, but also to an interest in using materials that have low embodied carbon."

TallWood has run dozens of applied research projects and initiatives, addressing everything from code issues to supply chain challenges to building performance to help get more advanced and engineered timber into use. The institute is part of the Oregon Mass Timber Coalition, a partnership between research institutions and Oregon state agencies that was awarded $41.4 million from the US Economic Development Administration's Build Back Better Regional Challenge. That funding is meant to back "smart forestry" and other research initiatives tied to increasing the market for mass timber.

Of course, part of the material's environmental promise depends on the back-end details, notably how and where the timber is harvested. Advocates of the sector argue that its expansion won't cause undue pressure on forests, in part because mass-timber products can be made from "low-value" wood—smaller-diameter trees that are already being culled as part of wildfire mitigation, diseased trees, and potentially even scrap lumber.

Conservation groups and other forestry experts are proceeding a bit more cautiously. The Nature Conservancy undertook a multiyear global mass-timber impact assessment in 2018, researching the potential benefits

Next: The 20-story Sara Kulturhus, a hotel and arts center in Skellefteå, Sweden, was built from wood harvested within a 35-mile radius of the city.

Below: A 1,200-seat theater at the Sara Kulturhus.

"Being in a wood building can just feel good."

and risks of increased demand for mass-timber products on forests, and is developing a set of global guiding principles for a "climate-smart forest economy"—best practices that will help protect biodiversity and ecosystems as the mass-timber market grows.

Often, builders and developers who specifically want to tout the use of mass-timber materials insist on sourcing that's certified as sustainable, according to Stephen Shaler, professor of sustainable materials and technology at the University of Maine's School of Forest Resources. "That demand is in the marketplace right now," he says.

Beyond an interest in sustainability, there's another reason for the proliferation of mass-timber projects: biophilia, or the human instinct to connect with nature. "Being in a wood building can just feel good," Shaler says. That's not just a subjective judgment; small studies have shown that wood interiors improve air quality, reduce blood pressure and heart rates, and can improve concentration and productivity.

Right: Interior of Sweden's Sara Kulturhus.

Opposite: The restaurant at Mjøstårnet, a mixed-use high-rise in Norway built from locally sourced mass timber.

The developers of the 25-story Milwaukee building, the Ascent, reportedly pursued the mass-timber approach largely for aesthetic reasons, and for the promotional value of its distinct look. Presumably the marketing payoff didn't hurt: as the tallest wood skyscraper in the world, the Ascent has been a centerpiece of mass-timber press attention. But there's another value to the public exposure: the 284-foot-high Ascent and other high-rise projects may not portend the future of all skyscrapers, but they demonstrate the possibility of safely building with mass timber at large scale. And that may help sway regulators and planners—particularly when it comes to approving the smaller-scale buildings that could be more important to proving mass timber's real potential. "The majority of the use is likely going be in the mid-rise, six- to eight-story kind of project," Shaler says.

The International Building Code permits wooden buildings up to 18 stories; the Ascent developers obtained a variance partly because their final design incorporated two concrete cores. As Sheine and Shaler both underscore, most mass-timber projects still incorporate at least some concrete, steel, or other materials. That's just fine, Shaler says: mass timber should be viewed as a comparatively new option that can help improve carbon footprints, not as a full-on replacement for traditional materials. And new options are always useful—even when they're as old-school as wood. ❯

Opposite: The Ascent in Milwaukee, currently the world's tallest mass-timber structure.

Below: Mass timber is increasingly used for multifamily structures and affordable housing developments, including Chiles House in Portland, Oregon.

IS WOOD THE WAY OF THE FUTURE?

THE LATEST

The 25-story Ascent in Milwaukee opened in late 2022, becoming the tallest mass-timber project in the world, and trade group WoodWorks counted more than 2,000 mass-timber projects around the world by the end of 2023. Meanwhile, research and development into new ways of working with the venerable material and improving its supply chain continues, notes Judith Sheine, an architecture professor at the University of Oregon and director of design for the TallWood Design Institute. Tallwood, UO, and Oregon State University are part of a joint effort gaining US Economic Development Administration backing to advance the mass-timber ecosystem in the Pacific Northwest, and TallWood is collaborating on mass-timber housing prototyping and facade retrofits for energy and seismic resilience. Recently, TallWood sponsored a Carbon Narratives for Design Planning report that took a comprehensive look at carbon in timber, particularly in mass timber. Among other conclusions, the report noted that while a significant shift toward mass timber could have a significant positive impact on carbon emissions, that scenario depends in part on forest management and land use—underscoring the importance of not just materials, but also the systems behind them.

LEARN MORE   **TallWood Design Institute** (Oregon State University/University of Oregon)
https://tallwoodinstitute.org

What Is the Impact of Mass Timber Utilization on Climate and Forests?
(The Nature Conservancy/USDA)
https://www.fs.usda.gov/research/treesearch/63853

Mass Timber Institute (University of Toronto)
https://academic.daniels.utoronto.ca/masstimberinstitute

E-BIKES EXPAND ACCESS TO ECONOMIC OPPORTUNITY

From a Black-owned
bike-sharing business
in Youngstown, Ohio,
to a Colorado program
that provides e-bikes
for essential workers,

new initiatives are making e-bikes
available in traditionally underserved
communities across the country.
These efforts are expanding
economic opportunity and shifting
longstanding perceptions.

Above: Shared Mobility team members visit Pacoima, California, during the pandemic to support the launch of an e-bike library.

Previous: Colorado State University provided 19 essential employees with new electric bicycles in 2021 as part of the state's Can Do Colorado e-bike pilot program.

WHEN THE FIRST commercial US bike-sharing program launched in 2008, the value proposition was clear. Putting more bikes on the streets was meant to reduce automobile usage and carbon emissions, provide urban residents and tourists with a flexible form of transportation, and offer a public health benefit to boot.

Over the next decade, bike-sharing quickly expanded across the country. But because bike-share programs often rely on corporate funding or are operated by profit-driven micromobility businesses, they've rarely been available in low-income neighborhoods or cities that would benefit from having access to more transportation options. Recently, this familiar pattern has gotten a jolt from the rising popularity of e-bikes—that is, bicycles equipped with electric-battery technology that supplements or at times replaces traditional pedal power—and from cities and cycling advocates putting different spins on the usual bike-share schemes.

Over the last couple of years, bike-sharing experiments geared toward lower-income residents and communities have launched or been announced in cities including Denver, Oakland, Buffalo, New York; Youngstown, Ohio; and Worcester, Massachusetts.

Sales of e-bikes are booming worldwide, and the technology is proving to be a game-changer. "All bike shares should be electric," says John MacArthur, sustainable transportation program manager at Portland State University's Transportation Research and Education Center (TREC), which released a report on the equity of bike-sharing in 2020. "I'm totally convinced of this."

The advent of the e-bike as a tool for expanding access to economic opportunity represents a chance to draw in more widespread popular support for transportation alternatives.

The key reason, MacArthur says, is that e-bikes have a track record of breaking longstanding barriers around who bikes. They attract older adults, people with physical limitations, individuals who haven't biked since childhood, and those who have never identified with the sport or culture of bicycling. With traditional bikes, he says, "you will only reach a certain number of people."

In cities like Portland, Oregon, and New York that have built out all-electric or primarily electric fleets, users "ride them farther and ride them more often," MacArthur says. A typical bike-share ride is about three and a half miles, TREC found; e-bike trips tend to extend beyond five miles, and approaching twice that isn't uncommon.

This can have a spatial and economic impact, potentially expanding access to neighborhoods, jobs, and services. Bike-share equity has become a recognized issue, and nonprofits and local entrepreneurs are stepping in to meet the needs of traditionally underserved communities and geographies. All the recent initiatives have at least the partial goal of not only expanding transportation options, but also providing the boost to neighborhood vitality and economic independence that can come with it.

Next: Unloading equipment headed for the Pacoima, California, e-bike library.

Below: Using demographic data related to age, race, and household income, researchers from the University of Delaware and Morgan State University developed a Bike Equity Index (BEI) in 2019 to evaluate how well Baltimore's bike-share infrastructure was serving the city's residents.

"Historical land use, banking, and other policies have led to a country with a very uneven geography of opportunity," says Jessie Grogan, director of Equity and Opportunity at the Lincoln Institute. "The correlation between neighborhood assets and racial and ethnic segregation was not accidental— so undoing it won't be either. While we need to work on making all neighborhoods places of opportunity, e-bikes can be an essential bridge between high- and low-opportunity places in the meantime. A cheap or free and convenient ride to another community for a good job, or a good school, or a recreational opportunity could be a lifeline for people in underserved neighborhoods."

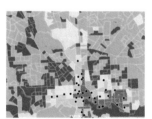
(a) BEI (%) vs. 39 Bike Share Coverage

(b) BEI (density) vs. 39 Bike Share Coverage

(c) BEI (%) vs. 57 Bike Share Coverage

(d) BEI (density) vs. 57 Bike Share Coverage

▮ Oversupply   ▮ Slight Oversupply   ▮ Balanced   ○ Full Build Bike Station
▮ Slight Undersupply   ▮ Undersupply   ● Current Bike Station

Shared Mobility, an equitable transportation nonprofit based in Buffalo, New York, is among the entities trying to help local partners fill the gaps. In 2020, the organization acquired about 3,000 e-bikes that Uber was planning to scrap after selling off its Jump-branded bike-share business. The group partnered with the city's East Side Bike Club (ESBC) to use some of the bikes to start an e-bike library in Buffalo, serving a low-income area with a predominantly Black population. E-bike libraries provide free bike rentals and bike-related education to community members; among other bike repair services and educational programs, ESBC now offers free weeklong use of its e-bikes. Shared Mobility has worked with partners in other communities in New York, California, and North Carolina to seed e-bike libraries in those places.

"While we need to work on making all neighborhoods places of opportunity, e-bikes can be an essential bridge between high- and low-opportunity places in the meantime."

Michael Galligano, CEO of Shared Mobility, says the kind of community engagement ESBC and other groups are involved in can help them land grants and funding to sustain these programs. But he also argues that bike and e-bike programs should be treated by municipalities as a form of public transportation—and both planned for and funded accordingly. "Where does public transit stop?" he asks. "We think it's not just buses and trains. It's also biking, walking, car-sharing, ride-hailing."

Galligano points to the Capital District Transit Authority, which serves Albany, New York, and surrounding municipalities, as an example of a longtime Shared Mobility collaborator that thinks this way—and will partially fund its own upcoming e-bike-share program with transit dollars. In Massachusetts, meanwhile, the state government has pledged $5 million to fund initiatives that make clean-energy transportation options like e-bikes more accessible to low-income populations; this will allow the city of Worcester to give e-bikes to 100 residents as part of a two-year study to learn more about the use and impacts of the technology.

Riders in Worcester, Massachusetts, where a multiyear pilot program run by MassBike provides e-bikes and training to local residents.

Another e-bike initiative in a legacy city is relying on a hybrid funding approach. YoGo Bikeshare launched in Youngstown, Ohio, this year with about 30 e-bikes distributed among four docking stations. The Black-owned business, funded by a loan from the Youngstown Business Incubator and an investment by its owners, is meeting a need in a city that other micromobility companies have passed over.

"Transportation in communities like Youngstown is a particular challenge, since decades of population and economic decline have led them to have very large and spread-out cities relative to their population size," Grogan notes. "Poorer cities are also generally not very well-served by transit, so it's particularly important to invest in mobility options in places like Youngstown."

The philanthropic community is also getting involved. MacArthur points to the work of Better Bike Share, a partnership funded by the JPB Foundation, which is working to increase access to and use of shared micromobility systems in low-income communities and communities of color. Its most

E-bikes have a track record of breaking longstanding barriers around who bikes.

high-profile city partner is Philadelphia; efforts there over the past decade to build a more inclusive bike-share system have set an example, MacArthur says, and Better Bike Share grants have now funded multiple projects across the country.

Clearly all these experiments are smaller-scale, incremental steps, not massive citywide transportation projects or comprehensive infrastructure overhauls. But incremental change can add up. At a minimum, the advent of the e-bike as a tool for expanding access to economic opportunity represents a chance to draw in more widespread popular support for transportation alternatives. And twinning the technology with neighborhood-level programs that double as community hubs, like ESBC in Buffalo, may be a useful way to reinforce that goal. Even if people are drawn in for recreation or pure curiosity, MacArthur says, that introduction can be a gateway to seeing e-bikes as a useful means of transport and can help inspire ambassadors to spread that message.

For more than a decade, most of the focus on bike-sharing programs was on decreasing vehicle miles traveled and carbon emissions while increasing profits. But an evolution seems to be underway, as access to bikes expands, perceptions begin to shift, and the economic and equity-related benefits of e-bikes become clearer. The goal of bike-sharing, Galligano says, is to add to the "repertoire of transportation options"—and if this new technology is inspiring fresh experiments and reaching new audiences, so much the better: "It's not one size fits all." ›

Opposite: Members of the East Side Bike Club head out for a ride.

Below: Global sales of e-bikes have grown steadily in recent years, and are expected to more than double during the next decade.

E-BIKE GLOBAL MARKET FORECAST (USD BILLION)

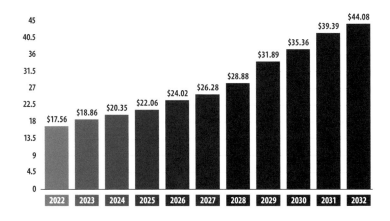

	2022	2023	2024	2025	2026	2027	2028	2029	2030	2031	2032
	$17.56	$18.86	$20.35	$22.06	$24.02	$26.28	$28.88	$31.89	$35.36	$39.39	$44.08

THE LATEST

Despite years of hype and investor enthusiasm, for-profit micromobility enterprises have had a rough ride lately; the high-profile scooter-sharing company Bird, for example, filed for bankruptcy late in 2023. That doesn't mean, however, there's no demand for such solutions. "It further emphasizes that public transit planners should look at these modes as part of their transportation models, and they should be publicly provided," says Michael Galligano, CEO of Shared Mobility. "These modes are highly used, they are just not that profitable—but they definitely turn out more revenue than buses." Shared Mobility continues to expand its work to help develop e-bike programs and encourage their integration into transportation systems, with new partnerships in Niagara Falls, New York, and an ambitious project in the Hudson Valley focused on underserved populations. Another promising development: a spate of local and state initiatives to lower the cost of e-bikes, often with a focus on low-income communities and individuals. This includes rebate and voucher programs in Portland, Atlanta, Denver, Washington, DC, and other cities.

LEARN MORE   **National Scan of Bike Share Equity Programs** (Transportation Research and Education Center)
https://trec.pdx.edu/research/project/1278/National_Scan_of_Bike_Share_Equity_Programs

Shared Mobility
https://www.sharedmobility.org

How Electric Bikes Could Stop Being a Luxury Item (*Washington Post*)
https://www.washingtonpost.com/climate-solutions/2023/10/05/ebike-rebate-voucher

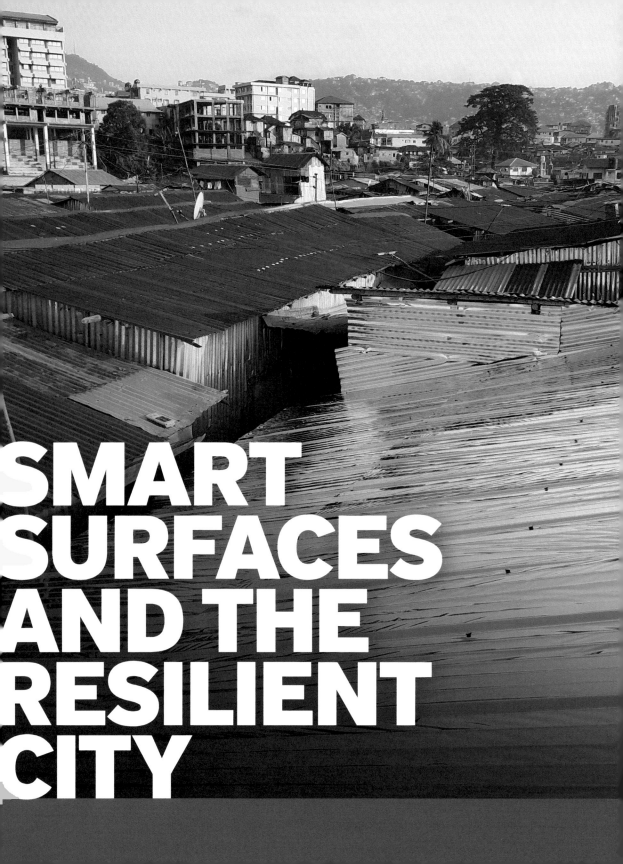

SMART SURFACES AND THE RESILIENT CITY

Roads, parking lots, and rooftops don't sound like the obvious site of innovative experimentation.

But the urgency of countering climate change is inspiring fresh creativity and invention when it comes to the materials used in these urban spaces.

Above: US cities including San Antonio, Los Angeles, and Phoenix (pictured) have added pavement coatings intended to cool streets and the neighborhoods around them.

Previous: Installing reflective film on a rooftop in Freetown, Sierra Leone.

A FEW YEARS AGO, the city of San Antonio, Texas, conducted research into the anticipated impacts of climate change on local temperatures. The study projected that, by midcentury, the city might experience 61 days a year with temperatures over 100 degrees. In reality, the city notched 75 days over 100 degrees—in 2023.

Like many cities, San Antonio has been strategizing responses to climate change for years, but recent record-shattering temperatures have given such efforts a new sense of urgency, says Douglas Melnick, San Antonio's chief sustainability officer. One major component that's been getting a serious rethink: city surfaces, from roads to roofs. These human-made surfaces are often dark and impermeable, amplifying hot weather and worsening flood risks, and contributing to the heat island effect. But soaring global temperatures are sparking a wave of experiments with new materials and engineering innovations designed to reimagine surface problems as deep opportunities.

Pavement is a particular focus for San Antonio and many other cities, because it's hot and there's a lot of it: researchers estimate that it accounts for 30 to 40 percent of urban land cover. After an initial "very small" pilot in 2021 experimenting with a reflective pavement coating, San Antonio embarked on a $1 million project that will test five such materials in

SMART SURFACES AND THE RESILIENT CITY

various parts of town, Melnick says. The streets were selected based on data related to equity and heat, and the work is being integrated into already-scheduled maintenance and repaving projects; the city will work with the University of Texas San Antonio to evaluate the results.

A similar effort is underway in Phoenix, a city "on the front lines of extreme heat," says David Sailor, professor and director of the school of geographical sciences and urban planning at Arizona State University. The city was an early proponent of rethinking surfaces, launching a major Cool Pavement Pilot Program three years ago. But even in this notoriously hot place, efforts have accelerated lately: ASU has been involved as a research and advisory partner in a city-led project that has treated more than 100 miles of local roads with reflective coatings. "This is something that would not have happened five years ago," Sailor says, "and it's increasingly happening across different cities."

Los Angeles has introduced a number of pilot programs, including one in the Pacoima neighborhood testing a reflective coating on streets, a school playground, and a recreation center parking lot. Researchers at Purdue University, meanwhile, have developed and are preparing for market the "world's whitest paint," which reflects 98 percent of solar heat and could be used on buildings, trains and buses, and other surfaces. A number of US cities are offering tax incentives for reflective roofs. Others have installed green roofs, topping waterproofing material with plants and other greenery that can be both cooling and absorb rainfall. And smaller projects are popping up all over the world, like parking lot solar canopies that provide shade and generate energy; corrugated self-cooling walls that stay as much as 18 degrees cooler than flat walls and can help reduce the need for air conditioning; and innovative, affordable cool-roofing materials for informal and self-built structures in India, Africa, and elsewhere.

The idea that governmental will to address extreme heat is expanding—and municipal

Above: Professor Xiulin Ruan led the Purdue University effort to develop the world's whitest paint, which was recognized by Guinness World Records and won a national SXSW Innovation Award in 2023.

Below and next: Thermal imaging shows the effect of applying solar reflective coatings to a basketball court in Pacoima, California, as part of the GAF Cool Community Project. The public-private partnership treated more than 700,000 square feet of streets, parking lots, and school grounds within a 10-block area.

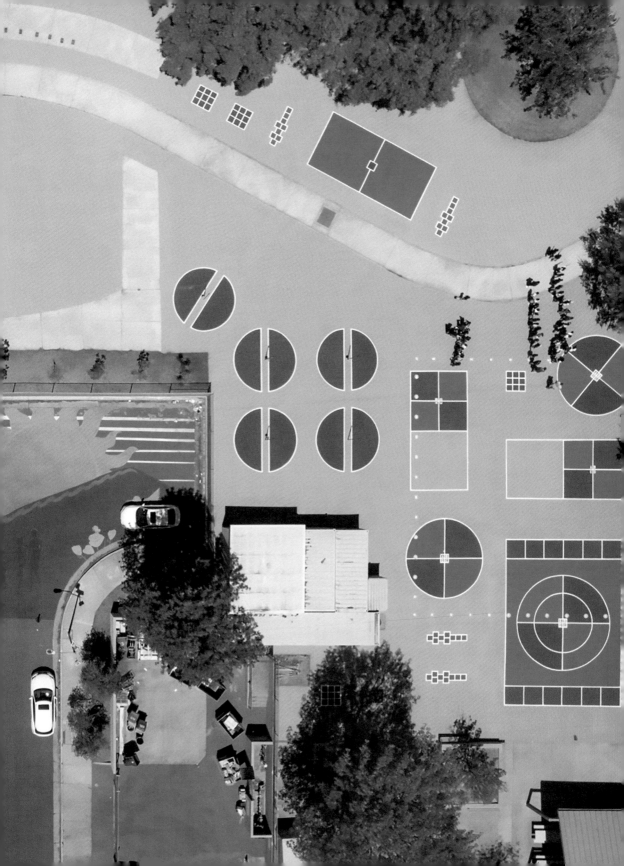

Preparing a reflective roof coating in Freetown. The material is part of a growing arsenal of tech-based approaches to cooling urban areas vulnerable to climate extremes.

funding is growing along with it—is spurring more material innovation in the market, says Sailor of ASU. He notes the creation of new, acrylic-based asphalt treatments. Because lighter colors can show tire markings, demand has also led to the development of coatings that are dark in the visible spectrum but engineered to have high reflectance outside that spectrum, and reflect 30 to 40 percent of the sun's energy, compared to 4 percent on a standard road. Other materials getting their moment in the sun include new kinds of coating for extruded metal roofing; reflective, porous concrete; and passive radiative cooling film engineered to actively radiate heat away from surfaces (instead of simply reflecting it, as coatings do). ASU is testing such products from giants like 3M as well as smaller startups.

But the real breakthrough isn't any single material or innovation, says Greg Kats, founder and CEO of the Smart Surfaces Coalition (SSC)—it's the sheer variety of projects afoot, and a new willingness to "think broadly and citywide" about surfaces. Launched in 2019, SSC is now working with some 40 organizations and 10 cities and metropolitan areas, providing data and tools to help implement smart surfaces effectively. "The city has gotten hotter and darker and more impermeable, with higher energy bills, more environmental injustice," Kats says. "A lot of cities have really reached a point where they're looking for systemic solutions." Kats notes that there are fiscal motivations, too: major credit rating agencies have begun to factor climate change into their calculations, which could affect municipal credit ratings.

Kats and other smart surface advocates emphasize that tech-based materials must be complemented by trees and other natural solutions. Brendan Shane, climate director for the Trust for Public Land, which focuses on

SMART SURFACES AND THE RESILIENT CITY

"The city has gotten hotter and darker and more impermeable, with higher energy bills, more environmental injustice. A lot of cities have really reached a point where they're looking for systemic solutions."

creating and enhancing parks and green spaces in cities and communities (and works with SSC), argues that smart surfaces and green infrastructure go naturally together. "Our tree canopies are at historic low levels," he points out. But they are part of a city's surface area, and "the surface of the city is one of those things that really does change. You're going to repave roads. And you're going to replant trees."

The coalition hopes to help cities devise multi-pronged but locally tailored approaches, Kats says, through improved data synthesis and analysis. SSC is already working with a dozen US cities, and two in India, to compile data from hundreds of sources, producing detailed heat maps from satellite data and other information, and running cost/benefit scenarios on different implementations and timelines. The goal is to be both comprehensive and flexible, given that a dry city like Stockton, California, will have different needs and solutions than a wetter city like Baltimore. Whatever a given city's objective, Kats asserts that with a full suite of responses—smart reflective surfaces, trees, and green infrastructure projects like rain gardens—the vast majority of cities can cool average temperatures by five degrees, or even more in previously neglected heat island neighborhoods.

Back in San Antonio, plans are taking shape to use heat-mapping technology to identify the neighborhoods that would most benefit from municipal investments in cool

The green roof at the Montgomery County Equipment Maintenance and Transit Operations Center in Gaithersburg, Maryland.

Right: Daytime surface temperatures far exceed daytime air temperatures and all nighttime temperatures, especially in downtowns and industrial areas.

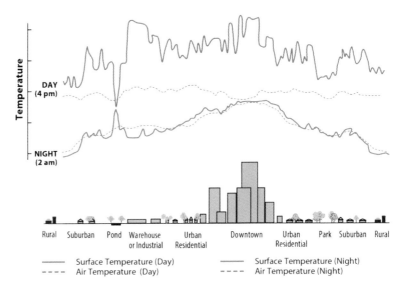

Temperature

DAY
(4 pm)

NIGHT
(2 am)

Rural Suburban Pond Warehouse Urban Downtown Urban Park Suburban Rural
or Industrial Residential Residential

Surface Temperature (Day)   Surface Temperature (Night)
- - - - Air Temperature (Day)   - - - - Air Temperature (Night)

Opposite: Researchers measure the reflectivity of cool pavement coatings at California's Lawrence Berkeley National Laboratory.

Below: Rooftops in Freetown covered with reflective coatings maintained an average temperature 25 degrees Celsius (77 degrees Fahrenheit) cooler than those without.

pavement, street trees, and shade structures. The wake-up call of recent extreme weather, Melnick says, has created a real opportunity for coordinated, citywide plans. "Cities tend to be very siloed. The parks department's doing trees over here, and then the public works department is doing roads over there," he says. "Everyone's got a role in mitigating heat, but how do we get everybody talking together?"

As technologies evolve and the world's cities continue to grow, investing in solutions to create cooler, more livable cities—and working together to implement them—is essential, Kats says: "Waiting is now a higher-risk strategy than taking action." ❯

THE LATEST

The urban cooling trend is continuing to gain momentum. A report from the Sabin Center for Climate Change Law at Columbia Law School notes that many cities are exploring how to use tax credits provided by the Inflation Reduction Act to help fund new smart surface projects. And as smart surfaces continue to emerge as an effective response to climate impacts ranging from intense heat to extreme storms, their rising profile has complemented more familiar calls for green infrastructure. Brendan Shane of the Trust for Public Land points to a 2024 study published in the journal *The Innovation* that links the urban heat mitigation potential of traditional solutions like street trees and parks with newer green engineering solutions like permeable pavement and green roofs. Meanwhile, work on the ground continues: San Antonio is expanding its citywide urban heat island mitigation effort, using data collected through a partnership with the University of Texas to focus its work on the most vulnerable neighborhoods. This $2 million project is expected to begin in 2024. The continued innovation in cities around the world demonstrates how quickly cities can move when they need to—and the likelihood of more record-breaking extremes is showing that the need is very real.

LEARN MORE

Smart Surfaces Coalition
https://smartsurfacescoalition.org

Cool Pavement Program (City of Phoenix)
https://www.phoenix.gov/streets/coolpavement

Smart Surfaces Guide (Carnegie Mellon University)
https://kilthub.cmu.edu/articles/report/Smart_Surfaces_Guide/20186438

BY GREG LINDSAY

So, what have we learned? Because the conflicts and collaborations compiled in this book are a mere dress rehearsal for the next wave of disruptions poised to crash upon cities, led by AI and climate change (which are increasingly entwined).

More important than the legacy of any single project contained within these pages are the overarching lessons ensuring we won't get fooled again.

First, governments must build their capacity to assess, deploy, and regulate urban tech. They should become comfortable with forecasting the impacts of nascent technologies before they pose a problem—or potentially hold the solution to pressing needs. For example, consider the contrast between the way Uber and Lyft ran roughshod over regulators for more than a decade and cities' far more proactive stance toward autonomous vehicles. Having internalized the former's externalities through increased congestion, reduced transit ridership, and higher pedestrian fatalities, cities have rightly kept a tighter grip on the wheel this time around.

Demonstrating this kind of hard-won wisdom, New York City passed a law overseeing the use of AI in hiring decisions just months after the launch of ChatGPT. Mayor Eric Adams quickly followed that by announcing a Department of Sustainable Delivery, which would be the first agency of its kind devoted to tackling the thorny issues raised by the skyrocketing number of e-bikes and e-commerce deliveries—including curb congestion and an epidemic of battery fires. But employers have overwhelmingly shirked the AI law, while even designated battery charging hubs have been fined for unsafe practices. There are still limits to what one city can do.

Which is why cities must work together to share tough lessons, find strength in numbers, and scale promising technologies. Now with more than 200 members in 40-plus states, Next Century Cities remains a model for joint advocacy on behalf of public infrastructure. It has since been joined by new peer networks such as the Open Mobility Foundation, an international city-led developer of open-source standards and software for managing vehicles and curbs. "You cannot negotiate with an Amazon or an Uber city by city," former Paris Deputy Mayor

Jean Louis Missika once told me. "You have to say the rules of the game are the same in Singapore and Paris."

The only way for cities to set those rules is to invest in building digital infrastructure themselves. One reason Sidewalk Toronto's cautionary tale still resonates is that the public-private partnership overseeing the project failed to define what it wanted from its Alphabet-backed vendor. While privacy concerns grabbed headlines, Waterfront Toronto's dereliction of duty is more troubling. When public agencies lack technical sophistication, they risk ceding control of public assets and data to private companies, which may prioritize profitable enclaves over inclusive deployment. Building public-sector capacity is critical to ensuring urban tech innovations benefit all residents, not just a privileged few.

> Building public-sector capacity is critical to ensuring urban tech innovations benefit all residents, not just a privileged few.

But it's also essential to do so democratically, in conjunction with residents, and this is where public officials and agencies have repeatedly stumbled—whether folding in the face of implacable NIMBYs or failing to persuade marginalized communities their best intentions aren't stalking horses for gentrification. CoUrbanize and pandemic-era virtual planning meetings hinted at the potential for new forms of cocreation, now being realized through generative AI tools such as UrbanistAI and Betterstreets.ai, which enable nonexperts to visualize exactly (more or less) what they want. Whether the matter at hand is new bus routes or bike lanes or berms against flooding, assuring public buy-in is crucial to meeting cities' climate goals in time for them to matter.

If the last decade of urban tech has been a dress rehearsal, then the curtain is now rising on the most momentous decade of change most cities have ever had to face. "Technology is the answer, but what was the question?" the British architect Cedric Price famously asked. Finally it is our turn to formulate what we demand from our technologies, versus the other way around.

———————

Greg Lindsay is a nonresident senior fellow of MIT's Future Urban Collectives Lab, Arizona State University's Threatcasting Lab, and the Atlantic Council's Scowcroft Strategy Initiative. He was the founding chief communications officer of AlphaGeo and remains a senior advisor. Most recently, he was a 2022–2023 urban tech fellow at Cornell Tech's Jacobs Institute, where he explored the implications of AI and AR at urban scale.

MY SINCERE THANKS to the scores of sources who took time from invariably busy schedules to share their expertise and patiently walk me through the practical details and big-picture implications of myriad subjects. Thanks also to the brilliant, generous, and unstoppable Maureen Clarke; I feel lucky to have stayed in your orbit all these years. Thanks to Katharine Wroth for perfect judgment and a sneakily reassuring sense of humor, and for always making me look better than I deserve. Thanks to Kevin Clarke for a dynamic and welcoming design that I hope the prose lives up to. Thanks to Kara Swisher for the opportunity to learn how it feels when a superstar writes your foreword. Thanks to Greg Lindsay for lending his trailblazing vision of the city's future(s) to this project. Thanks to Emily McKeigue for masterful masterminding, and to Amy Finch, Anthony Flint, Jon Gorey, and Jennifer Sigler for instrumental editorial and design input. Thanks to Kristina McGeehan and Catherine Benedict for getting the book in front of the right audiences, and to Heather Dubnick and Hannah Frith for invaluable contributions. Thanks to the Lincoln Institute of Land Policy for trusting me to contribute to its admirable and vital mission. And thank you, again and again, and always, and for everything, to E.

CHAPTER 12: NEW APPS ENCOURAGE CLIMATE POSITIVE DESIGN

116, 118: Climate Positive Design/CMG Landscape Architecture; 119, 120: CMG Landscape Architecture; 122: Building Transparency; 123, 124: Climate Positive Design/CMG Landscape Architecture; 125: Brandon Huttenlocher/Design Workshop.

CHAPTER 13: LATIN AMERICA AND THE E-BUS REVOLUTION

126: METBUS via C40; 128: Agência Brasília/Flickr CC BY 2.0; 129: E-BUS RADAR (top), Tamara Merino (bottom); 130: REUTERS/Ivan Alvarado; 131: Courtesy of Yutong Bus Co., Ltd.; 132: Tamara Merino; 134: Xinhua/Alamy Stock Photo; 135: REUTERS/Toby Melville (top), Aliaksandr Baiduk/Alamy Stock Photo (middle), kaprik / Alamy Stock Photo (bottom); 136: REUTERS/Ivan Alvarado; 137: Tamara Merino.

CHAPTER 14: MANAGING THE CURB

138: ©Dylan Passmore; 140: City of Raleigh/NACTO/Flickr CC BY-NC 2.0; 141: Courtesy of UCLA Luskin School (left), courtesy of Urban Freight Lab (right); 142: EXTREME-PHOTOGRAPHER/iStock/Getty Images Plus; 144: Mona Shield Payne for Cox Communications, Las Vegas; 145: ©2024 Esri and its data contributors. All rights reserved. Used with permission; 146: Kelsey Brunner/Aspen Times; 147: Jillian Forstadt/90.5 WESA.

CHAPTER 15: AS DELIVERY METHODS EVOLVE, WILL CITY STREETS KEEP UP?

148: Mandi Wright–USA TODAY NETWORK; 150: Courtesy of Nuro; 151: ©2019 MLive Media Group. All rights reserved. Used with permission; 152: Courtesy of Starship Technologies; 154: Oldenberg Design/Cornell Tech; 155: Robert K. Chin/Alamy Stock Photo; 156: Sean Davis/ Flickr CC BY-ND 2.0; 157: MediaProduction/iStock/Getty Images Plus.

CHAPTER 16: DESIGNING DASHBOARDS FOR LOCAL CLIMATE GOALS

158: Ken Batts; 160: Wiskerke/Alamy Stock Photo; 161: Metropolitan Council, Twin Cities; 162: Leila Navidi/Star Tribune via AP; 164: Cesareo Contreras–USA TODAY NETWORK; 165: Courtesy photo; 166: Metropolitan Area Planning Council, Boston; 167: Brian P. Smyla/ Windtech via Wikimedia Commons.

CHAPTER 17: NEW ANGLES ON NOISE POLLUTION

168: kyoshino/iStock/Getty Images Plus; 170: Jeffrey Isaac Greenberg/Alamy Stock Photo; 171: Mike Albans/NY Daily News Archive via Getty Images; 172: Courtesy of Bruitparif; 174: Courtesy of Harvard TH Chan School of Public Health; 175: Courtesy of Bruitparif; 176: Jordi Boixareu/Alamy Stock Photo; 177: Courtesy of Naturawall.

CHAPTER 18: IS WOOD THE WAY OF THE FUTURE?

178: Photography: Kyle Jeffers, Project: Perkins&Will; 180: Photography: ©Albert Vecerka/ Esto, Architecture: Leers Weinzapfel Associates; 181: Courtesy of BigRentz.com; 182: Photography: ©Albert Vecerka/Esto, Architecture: Leers Weinzapfel Associates; 183: SSEA;

184: Sven Burman/Unsplash; 186: Loulou d'Aki; 187: Moelven; 188: Courtesy of Holmes US; 189: CoStar Group/New Land Enterprises.

CHAPTER 19: E-BIKES EXPAND ACCESS TO ECONOMIC OPPORTUNITY

190: John Eisele, Colorado State University; 192: Patrick Cray/Shared Mobility; 193: Bhuyan, Istiak A., Celeste Chavis, Amirreza Nickkar, and Philip Barnes. 2019. "GIS-Based Equity Gap Analysis: Case Study of Baltimore Bike Share Program," *Urban Science. 3*(2): 42. https://doi.org/10.3390/urbansci3020042. 194: Patrick Cray/Shared Mobility; 196: MassBike; 198: Precedence Research; 199: East Side Bike Club.

CHAPTER 20: SMART SURFACES AND THE RESILIENT CITY

200: Dr. Ye Tao/MEER (MEER.org); 202: City of Phoenix Street Transportation; 203: Purdue University (top), Sunjay Lee/GAF Cool Community Project (bottom); 204: Sunjay Lee/GAF Cool Community Project; 206: Dr. Ye Tao/MEER (MEER.org); 207: Montgomery County (Md.) Department of General Services; 208: US Environmental Protection Agency (top), Dr. Ye Tao/MEER (MEER.org) (bottom); 209: Roy Kaltschmidt/Berkeley Lab, ©2012 The Regents of the University of California, Lawrence Berkeley National Laboratory.

INSIDE BACK COVER

Elizabeth Pagliacolo; Climate Positive Design/CMG Landscape Architecture; Yutong Bus Co., Ltd.; City of Raleigh/NACTO/Flickr CC BY-NC 2.0; Courtesy of Starship Technologies; Brian P. Smyla/Windtech via Wikimedia Commons; Courtesy of Naturawall; Sven Burman/Unsplash; MassBike; Purdue University.

BACK COVER

REUTERS/Toby Melville (top left); courtesy of Bruitparif (top right); Roy Kaltschmidt/Berkeley Lab, ©2012 The Regents of the University of California, Lawrence Berkeley National Laboratory (bottom).

INDEX

ABOUT THE AUTHOR

Rob Walker is a journalist and columnist covering technology, design, business, and other subjects. A longtime contributor to the *New York Times*, Walker writes a column on branding for *Fast Company,* and has contributed to *Bloomberg Businessweek*, the *Atlantic, Fortune, Marketplace,* and many other outlets. He writes the City Tech column for *Land Lines*, the magazine of the Lincoln Institute of Land Policy. Walker is the coeditor of *Lost Objects: 50 Stories About the Things We Miss and Why They Matter,* and the author of *The Art of Noticing*. His *Art of Noticing* newsletter is at robwalker.substack.com. He serves on the faculty of the School of Visual Arts in New York City.

ABOUT THE LINCOLN INSTITUTE OF LAND POLICY

The Lincoln Institute of Land Policy seeks to improve quality of life through the effective use, taxation, and stewardship of land. A nonprofit private operating foundation whose origins date to 1946, the Lincoln Institute researches and recommends creative approaches to land as a solution to economic, social, and environmental challenges. Through education, training, publications, and events, we integrate theory and practice to inform public policy decisions worldwide. We organize our work around three impact areas of land policy: land and water, land and fiscal systems, and land and communities. We envision a world where cities and regions prosper and benefit from coordinated land use planning and public finance; where communities thrive due to efficient and equitable allocation of limited land resources; and where stewardship of land and water resources ensures a livable future. We work globally, with locations in Cambridge, Massachusetts; Washington, DC; Phoenix, Arizona; and Beijing, China.